TABLE OF CONTE

C000098924

Alligator (572 dots) - Black

DOT TO DOT
SEA CREATURES
FOR ADULTS

This book includes 30 Unique Dot Pages, each dot page is included twice, first with dark BLACK numbers and second one with GRAY numbers.

Start from 1st Number dot and continue all the way till you reach end of numbers, all the designs are continous lines and there are no jumps or breaks!

If you have any suggestions or ideas, please drop an email to info@coloringbooks101.com

Copyright © 2021 by Sonia Rai

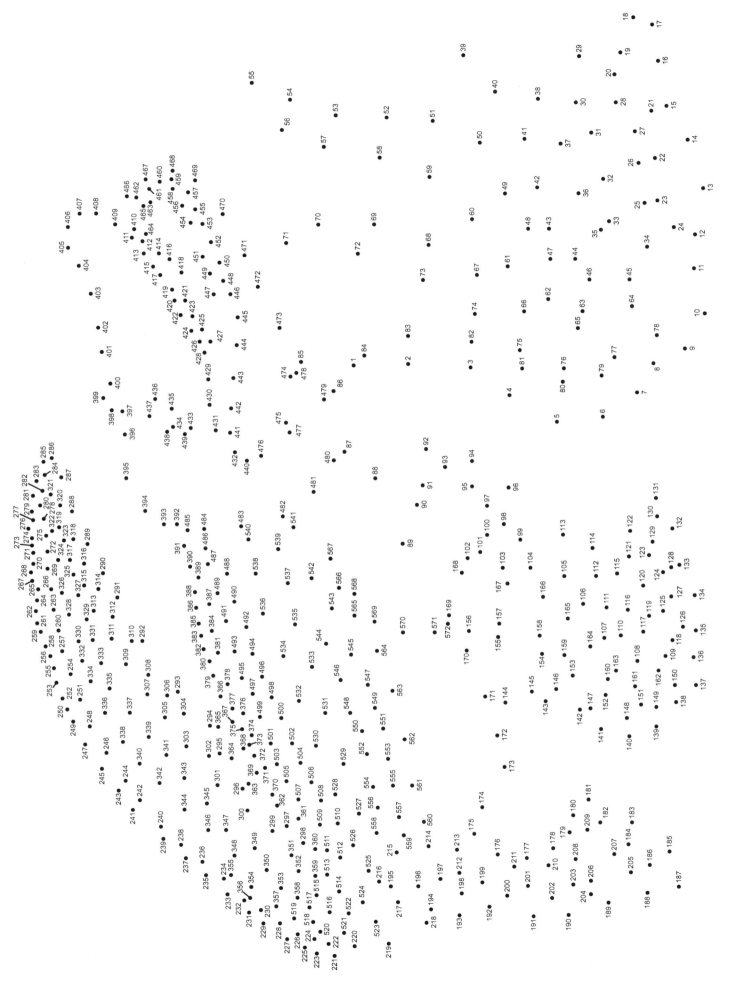

Alligator (572 dots) - Gray

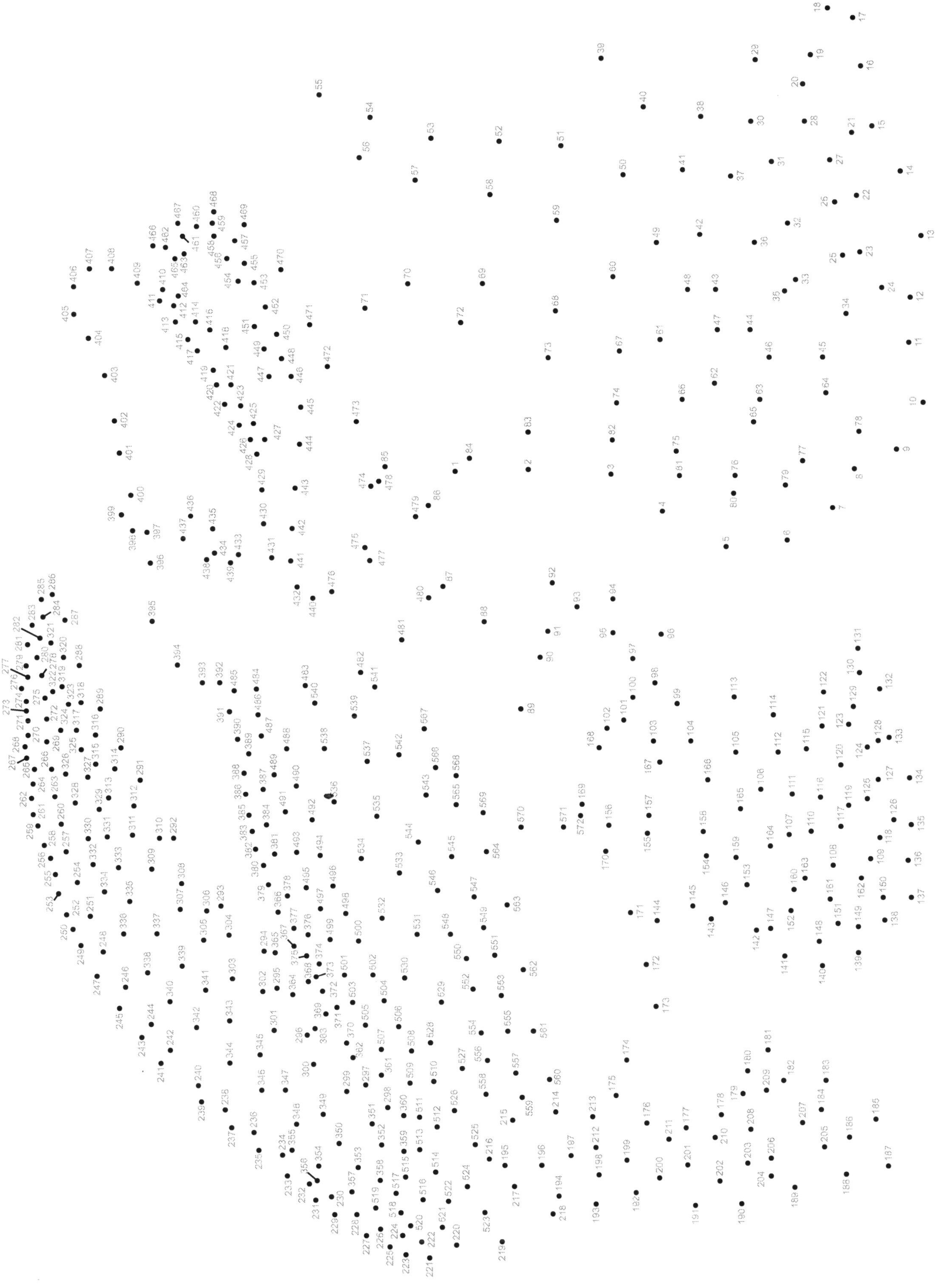

Clownfish (610 dots) - Black

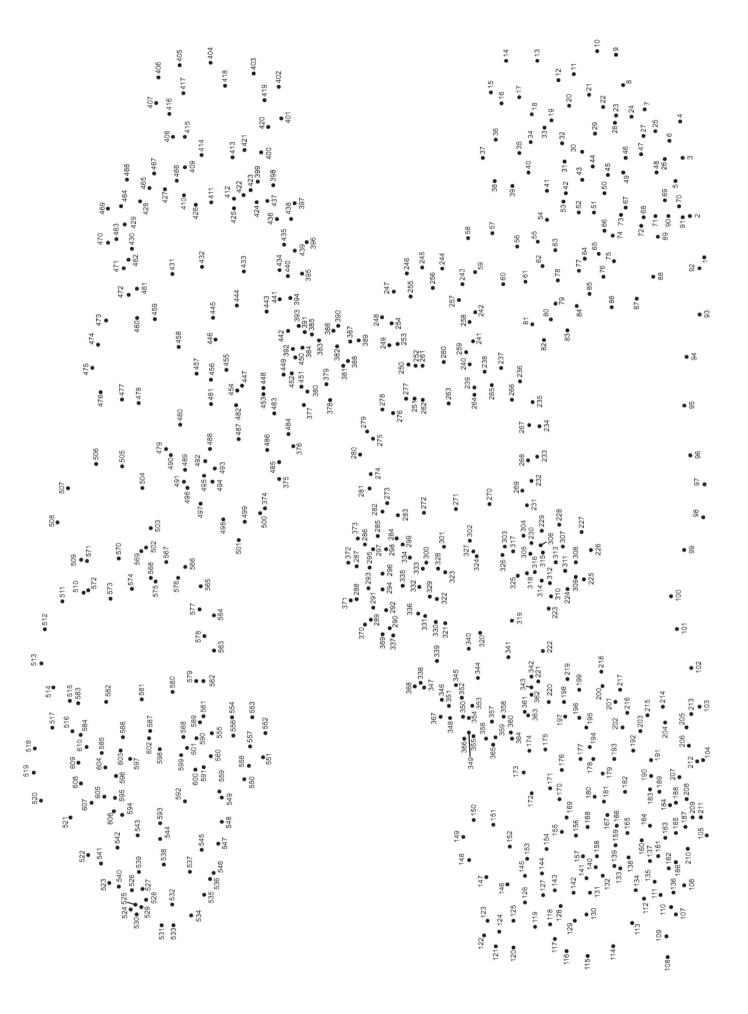

Clownfish (610 dots) - Gray

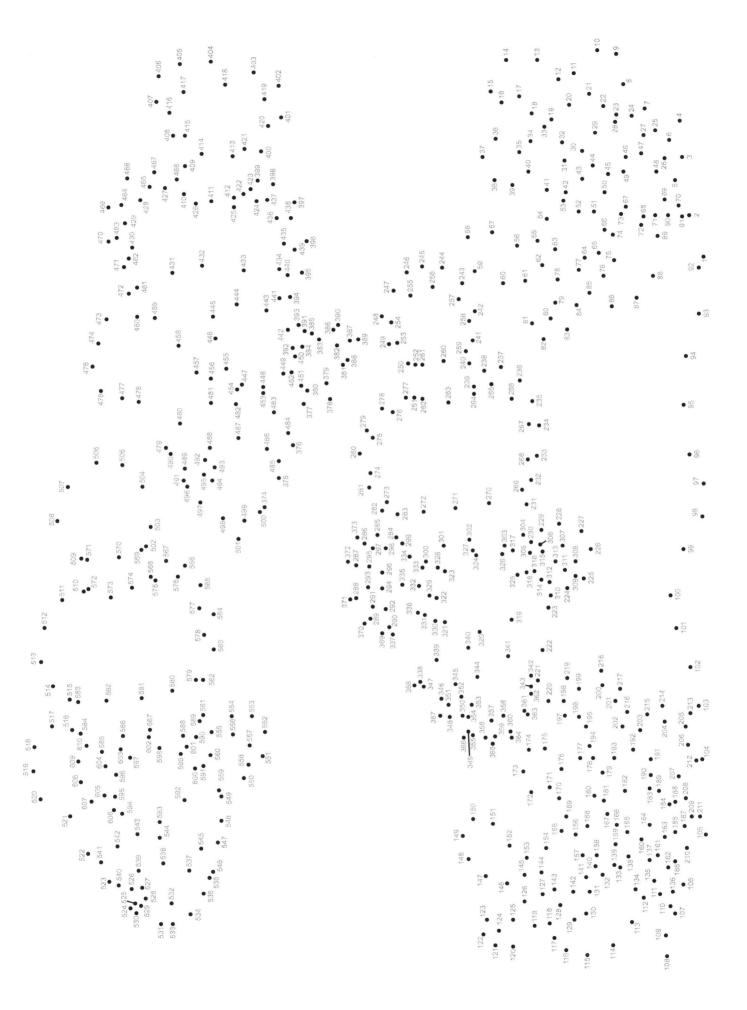

Crab (460 dots) - Black

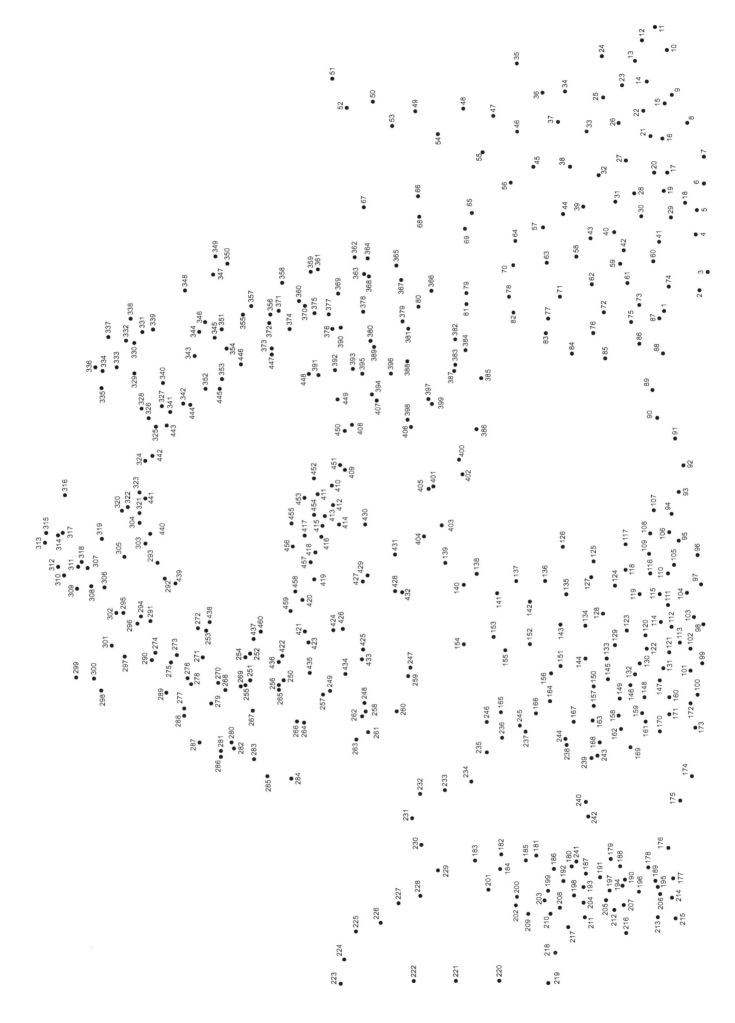

Crab (460 dots) - Gray

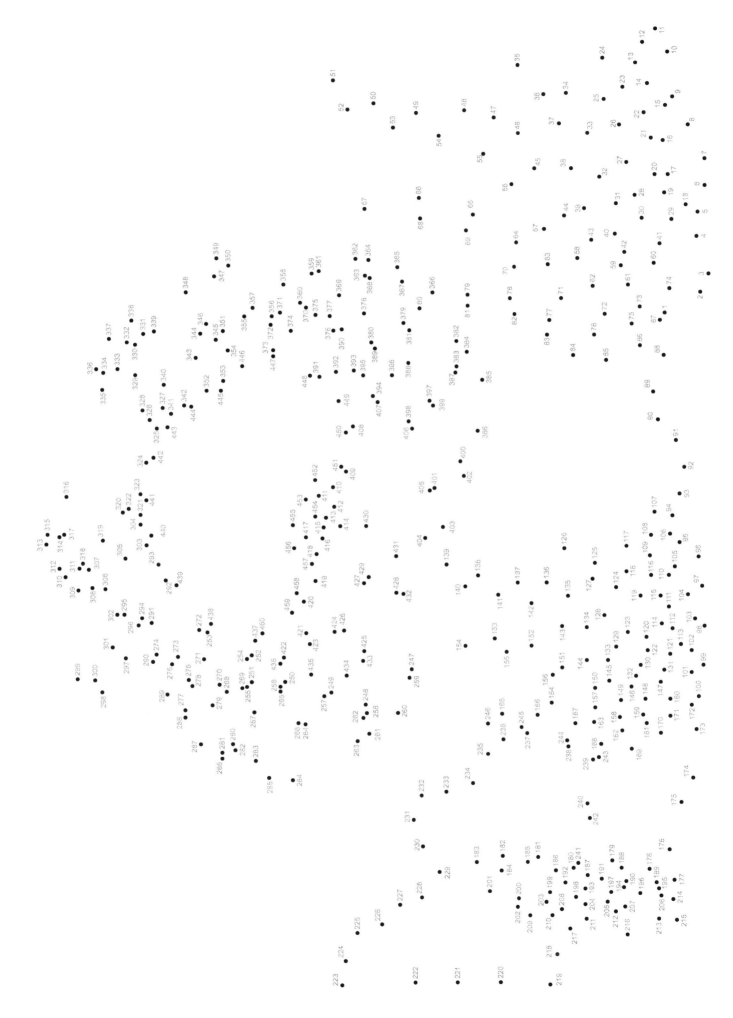

Cuttlefish (571 dots) - Black

Cuttlefish (571 dots) - Gray

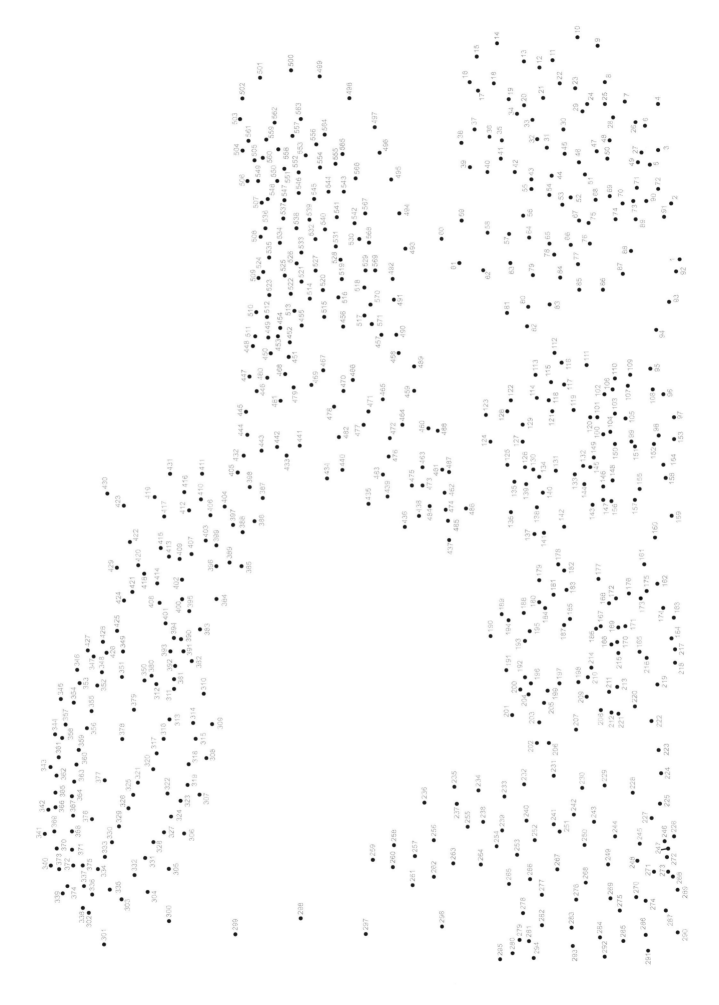

Dolphin (377 dots) - Black

Dolphin (377 dots) - Gray

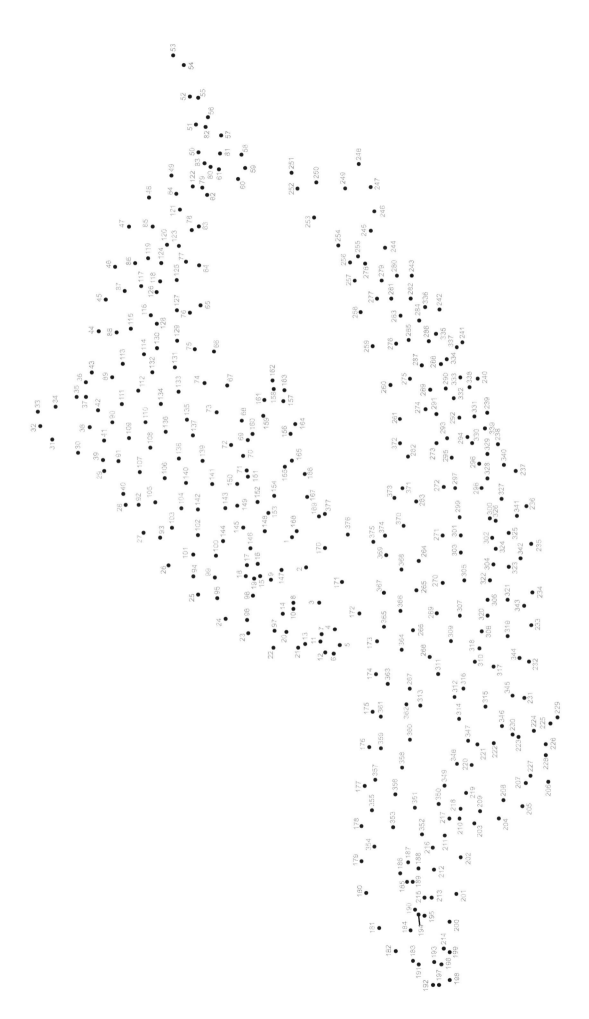

Electric Ele (445 dots) - Black

Electric Ele (445 dots) - Gray

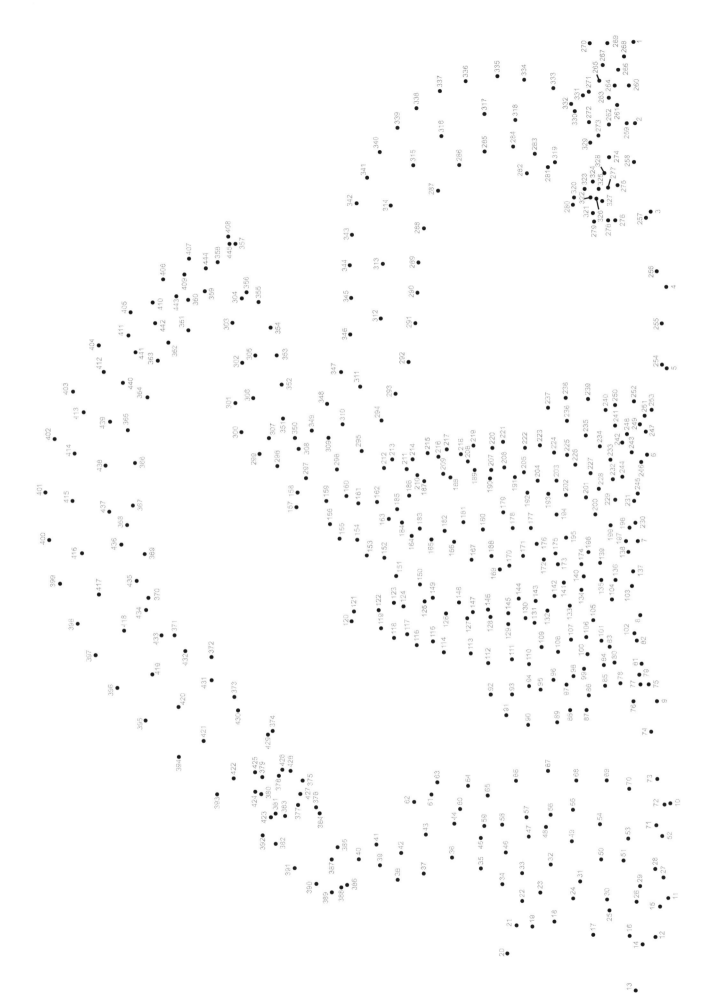

Frog (555 dots) - Black

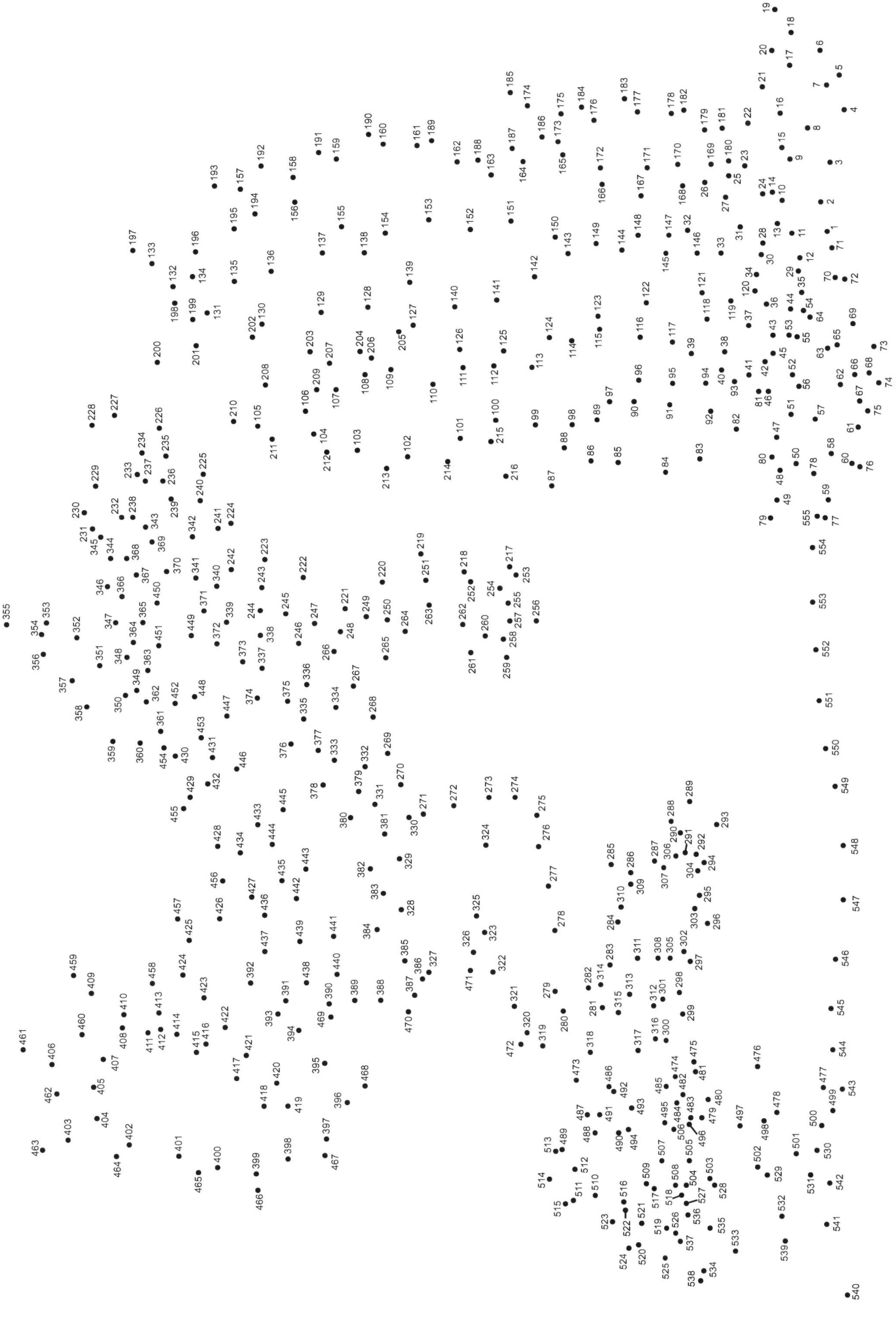

Frog (555 dots) - Gray

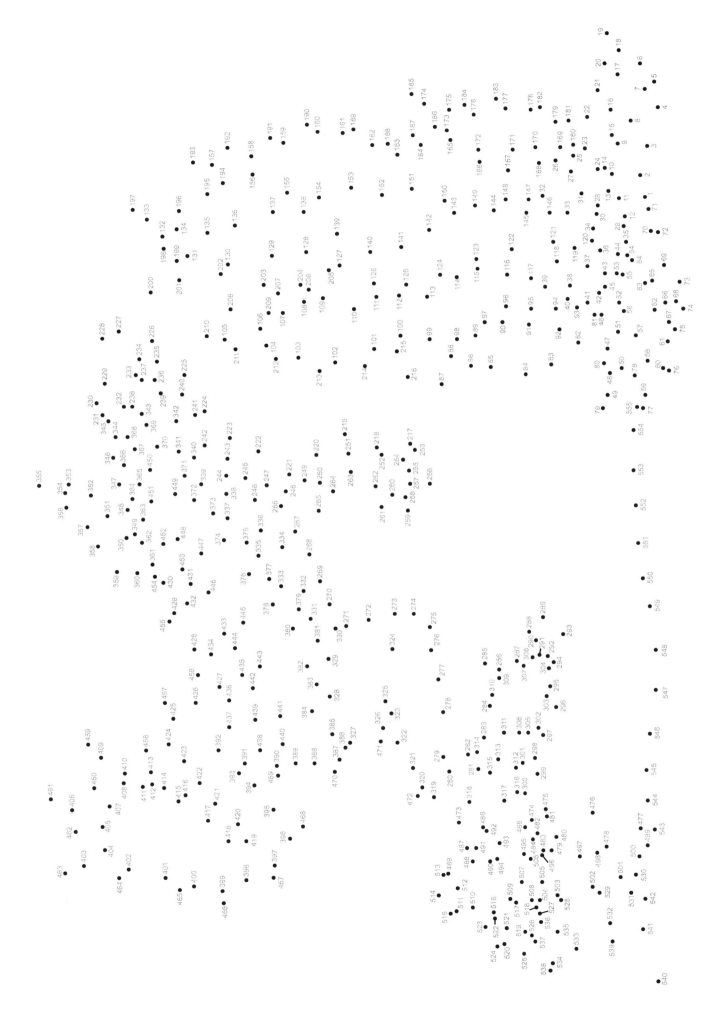

Garfish (576 dots) - Black

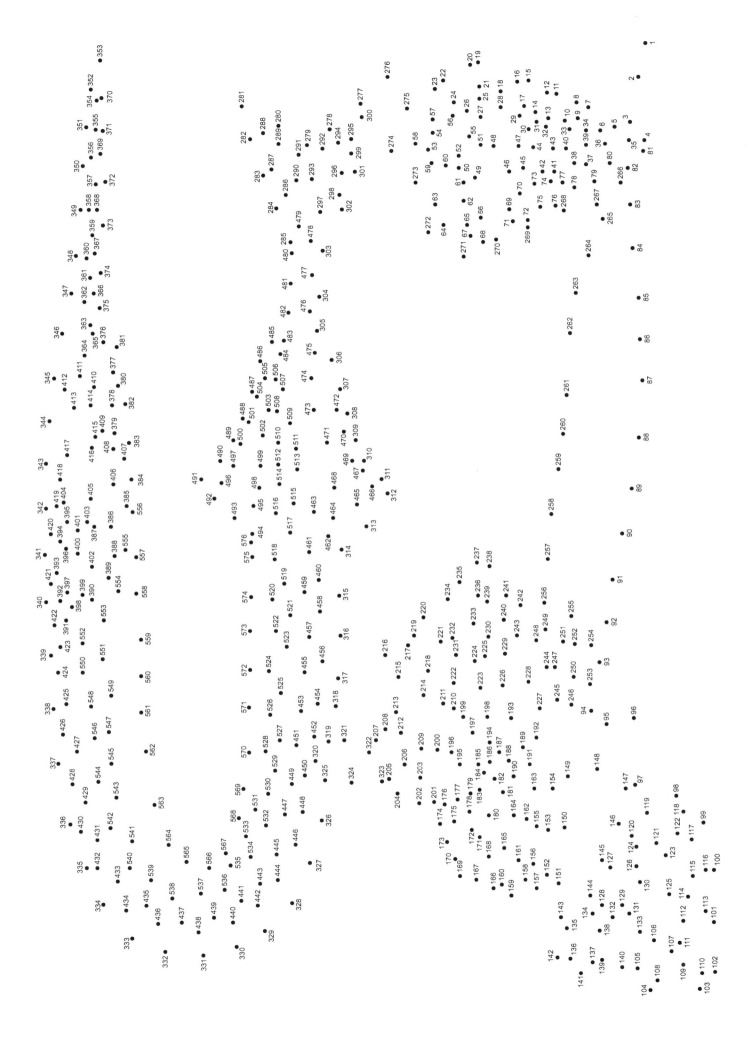

Garfish (576 dots) - Gray

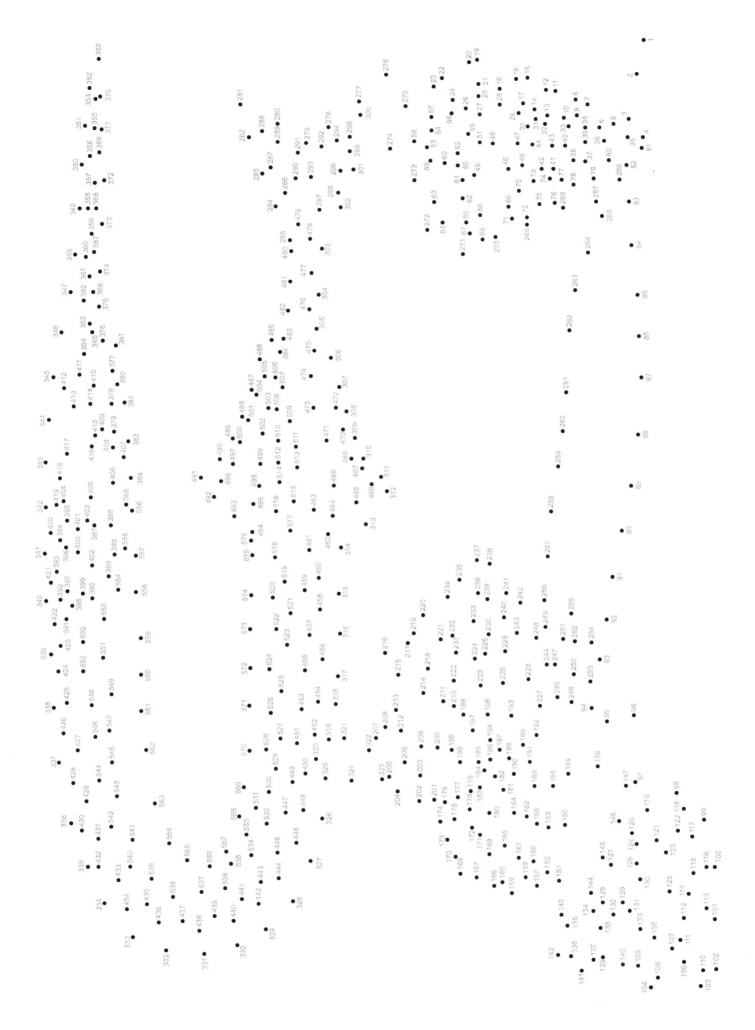

Goldfish (773 dots) - Black

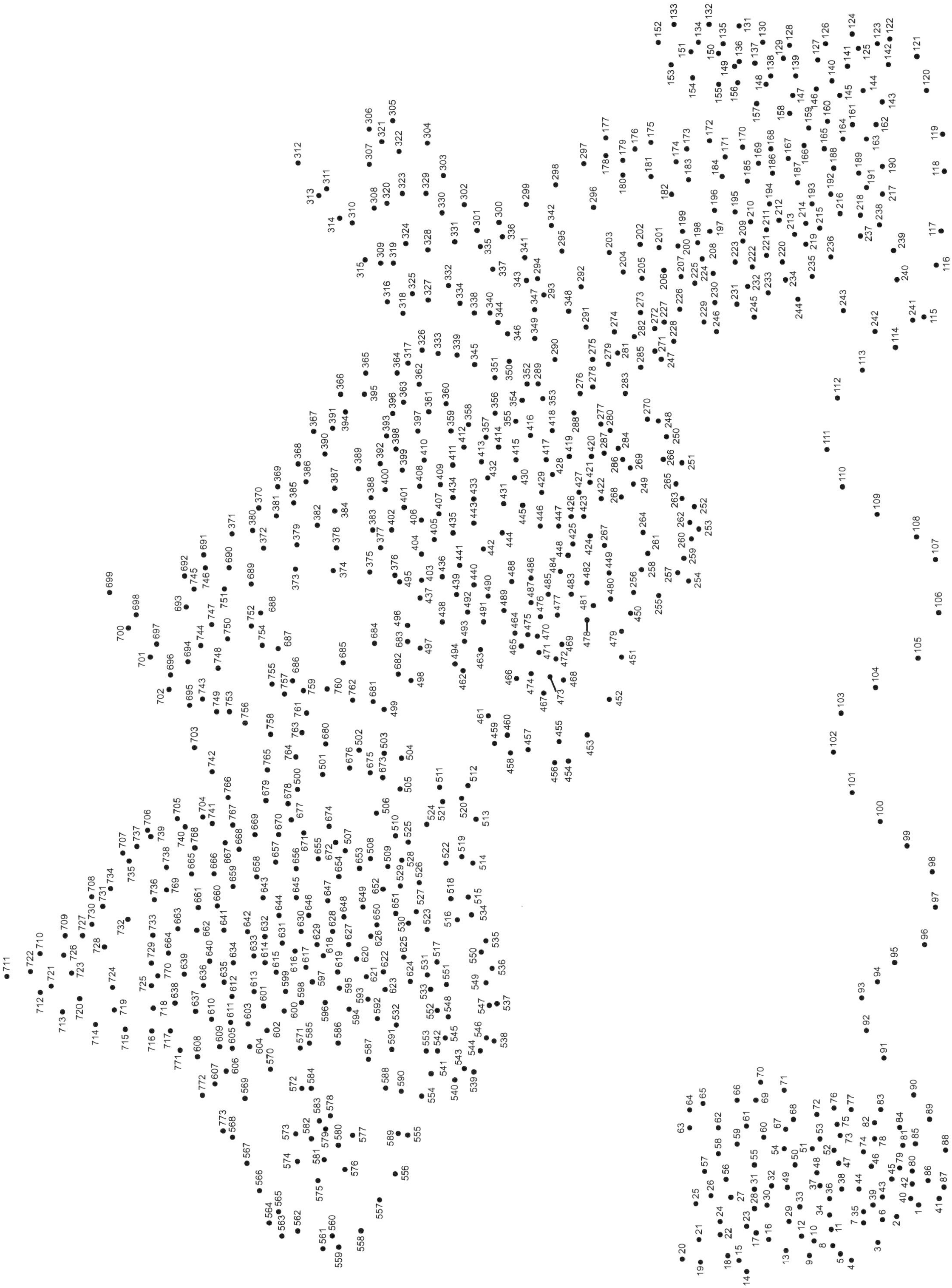

Goldfish (773 dots) - Gray

Guppy (612 dots) - Black

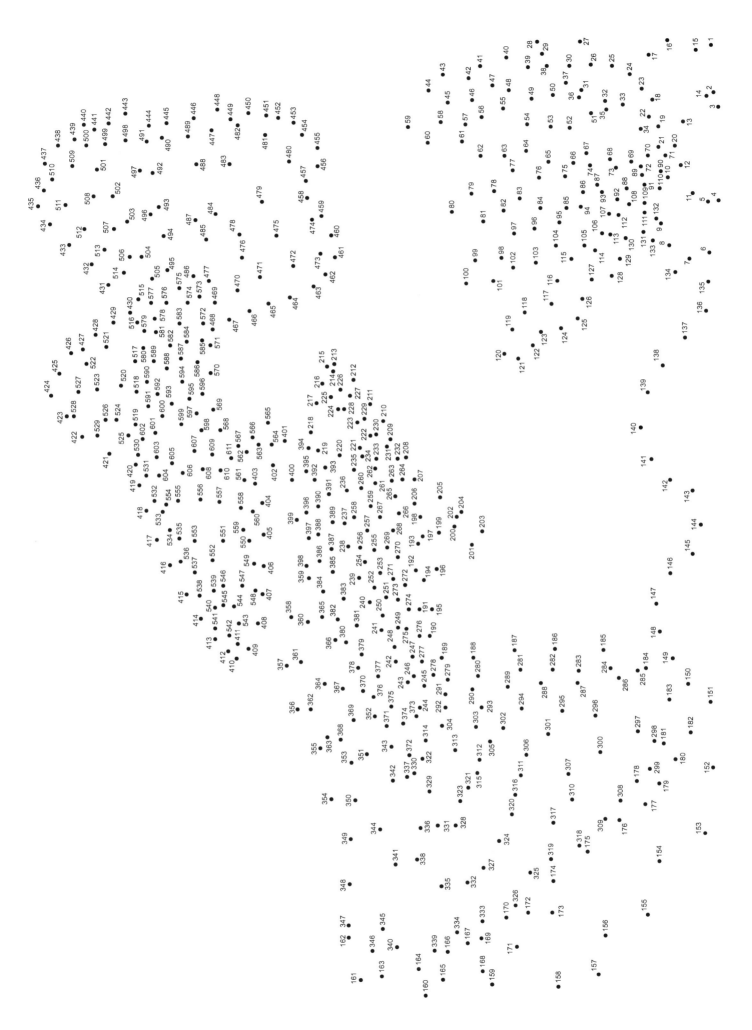

Guppy (612 dots) - Black

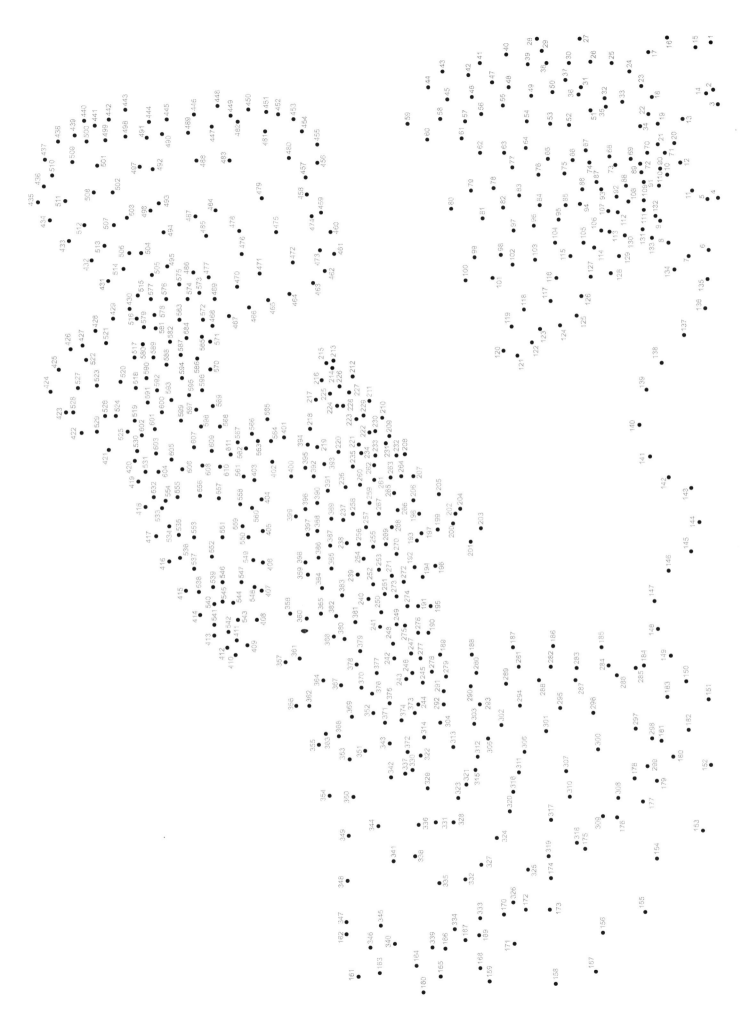

Humpback Whale (656 dots) - Black

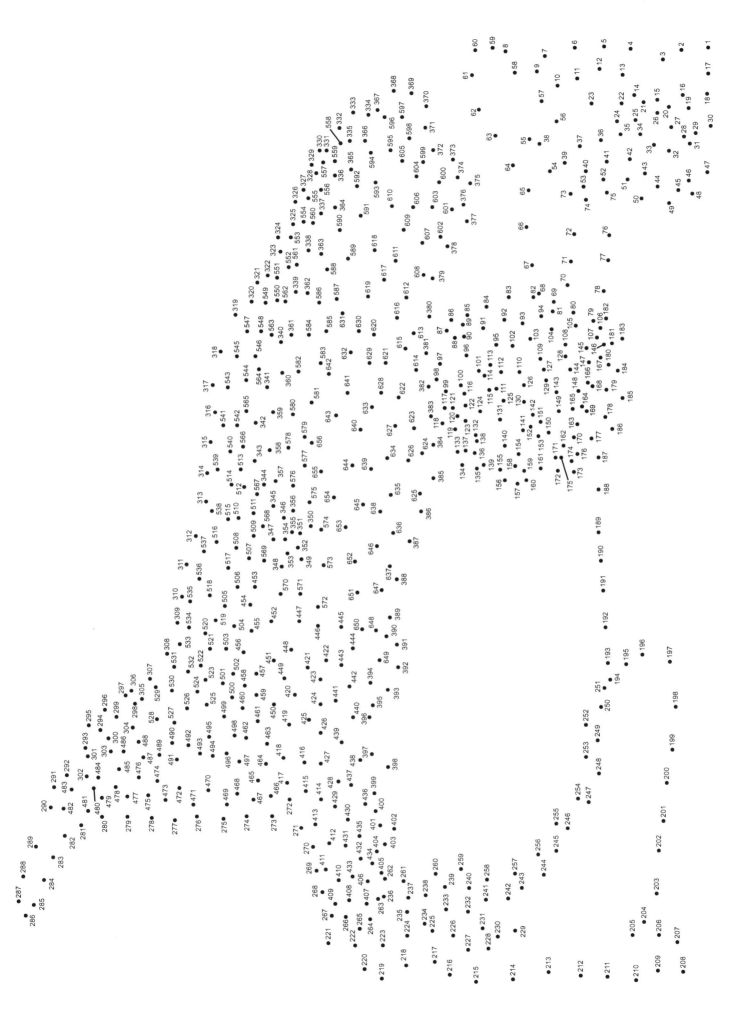

Humpback Whale (656 dots) - Gray

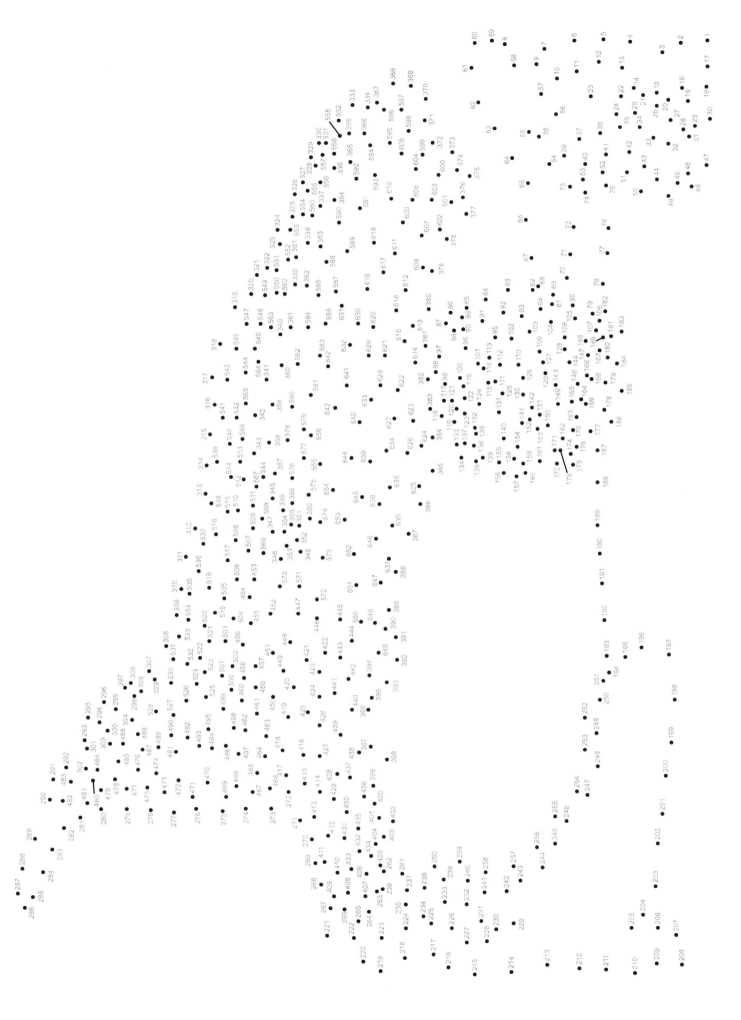

Jellyfish (420 dots) - Black

Jellyfish (420 dots) - Gray

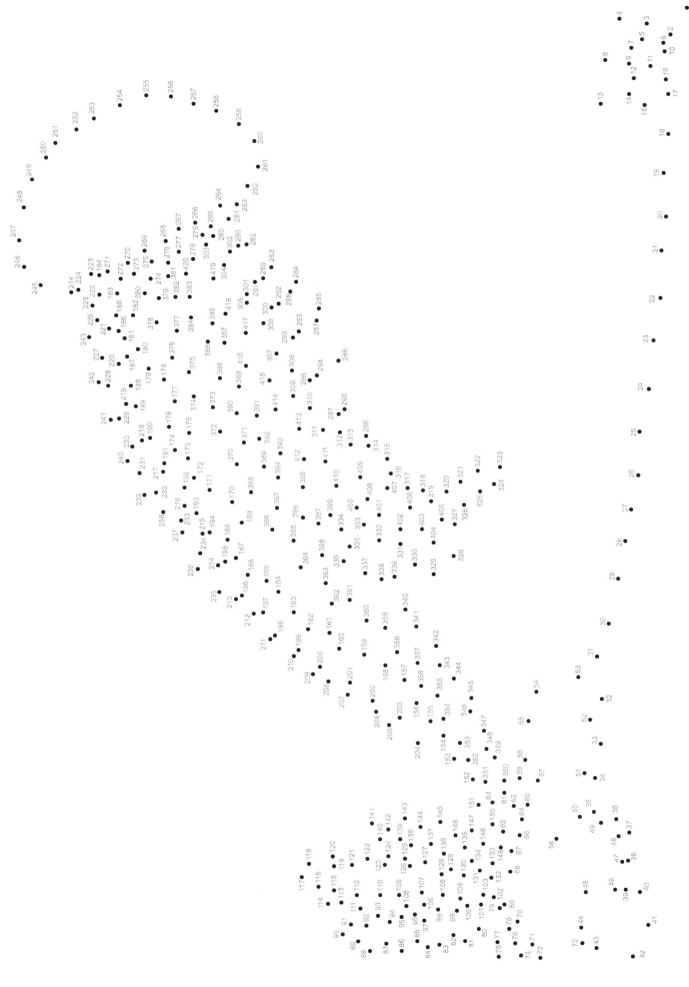

Lobster (313 dots) - Black

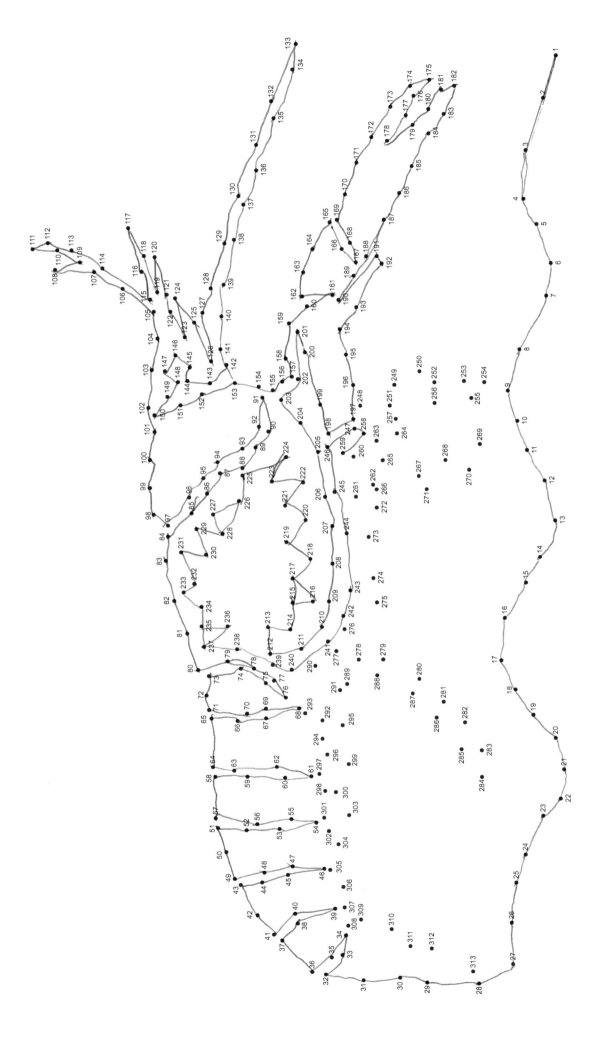

Lobster (313 dots) - Gray

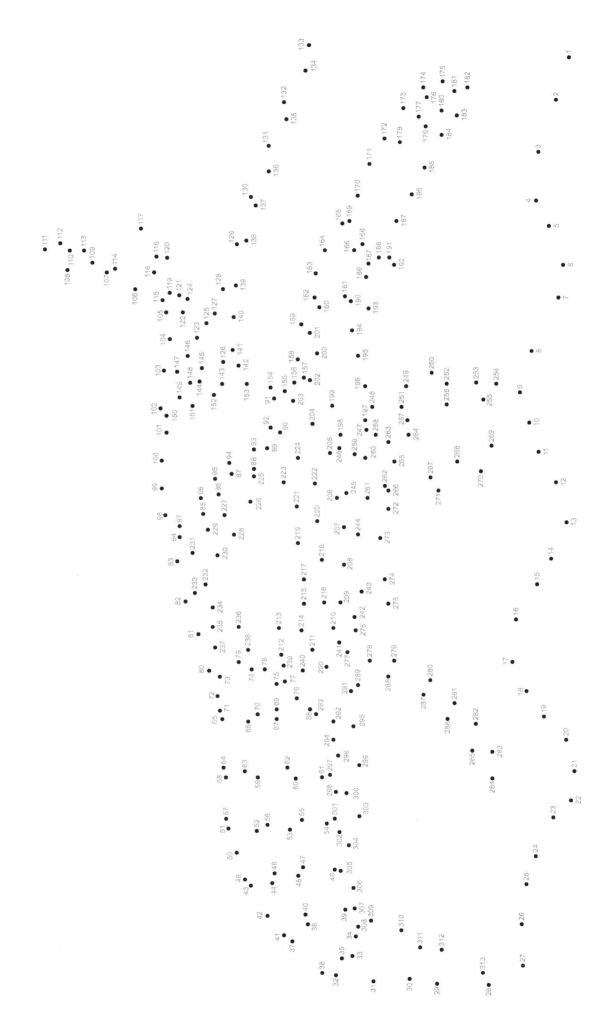

Marine Angelfish (728 dots) - Black

Marine Angelfish (728 dots) - Gray

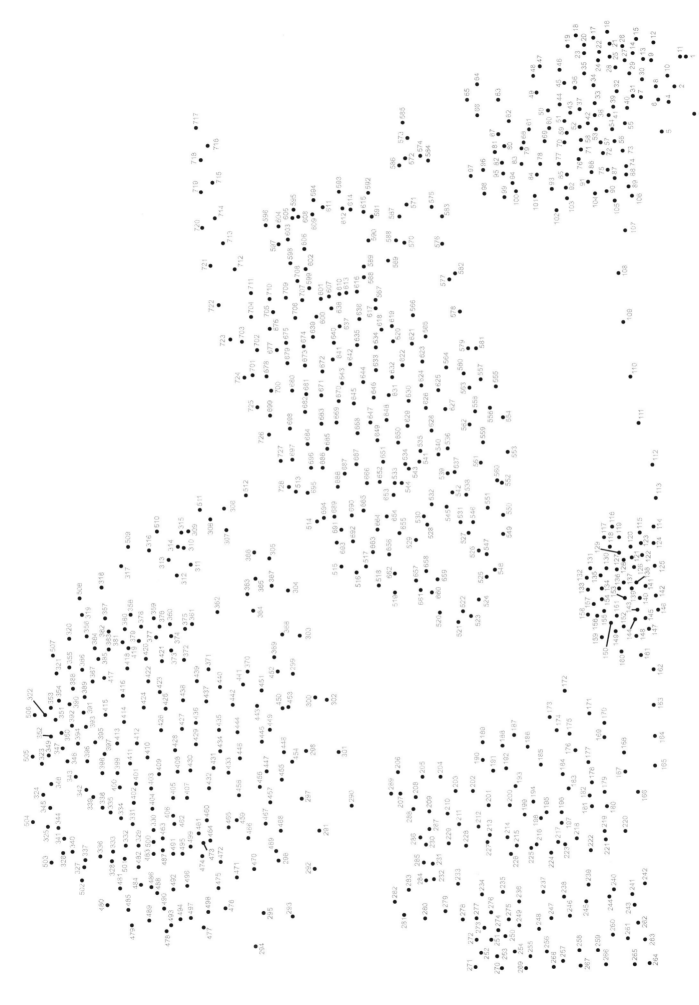

Octopus (483 dots) - Black

Octopus (483 dots) - Gray

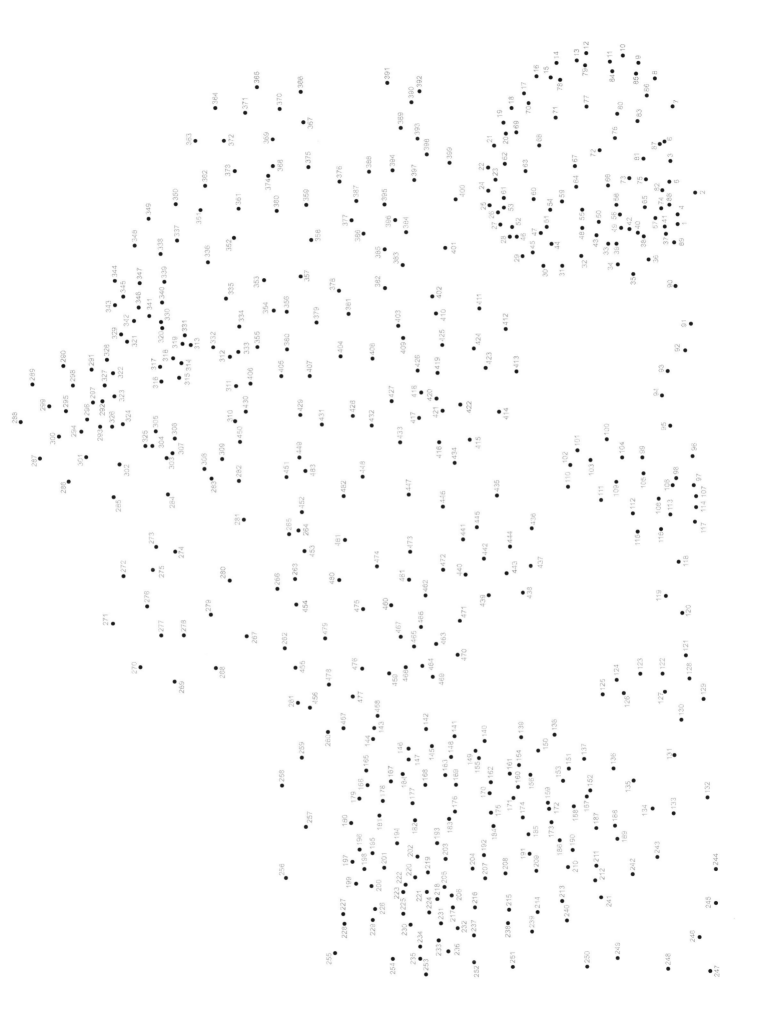

Orca (537 dots) - Black

Orca (537 dots) - Gray

Otter (528 dots) - Black

Otter (528 dots) - Gray

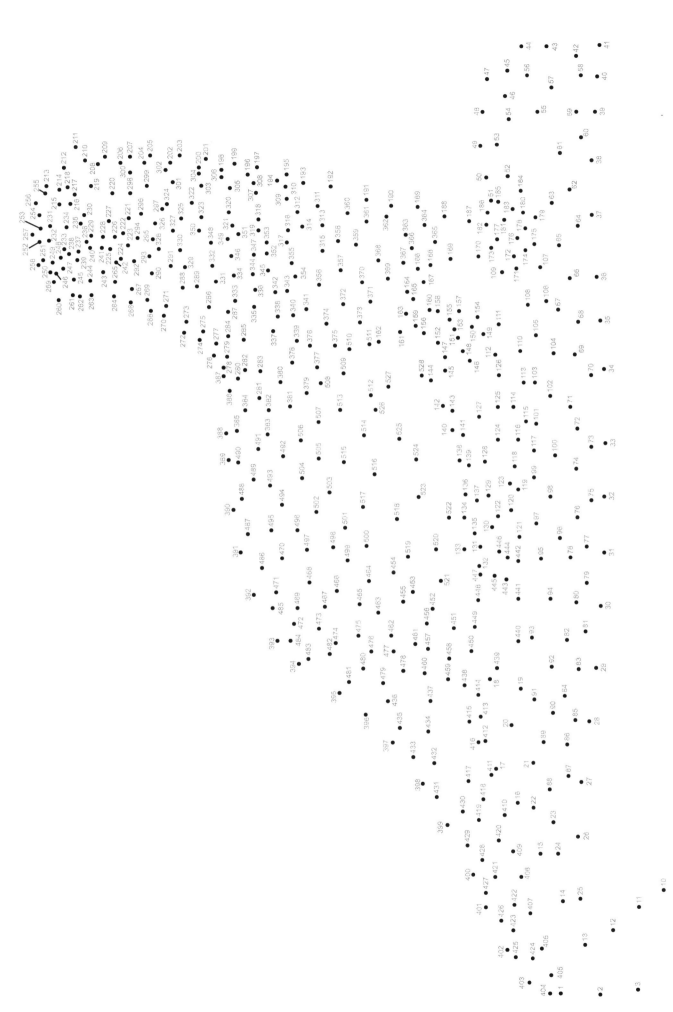

Penguin (514 dots) - Black

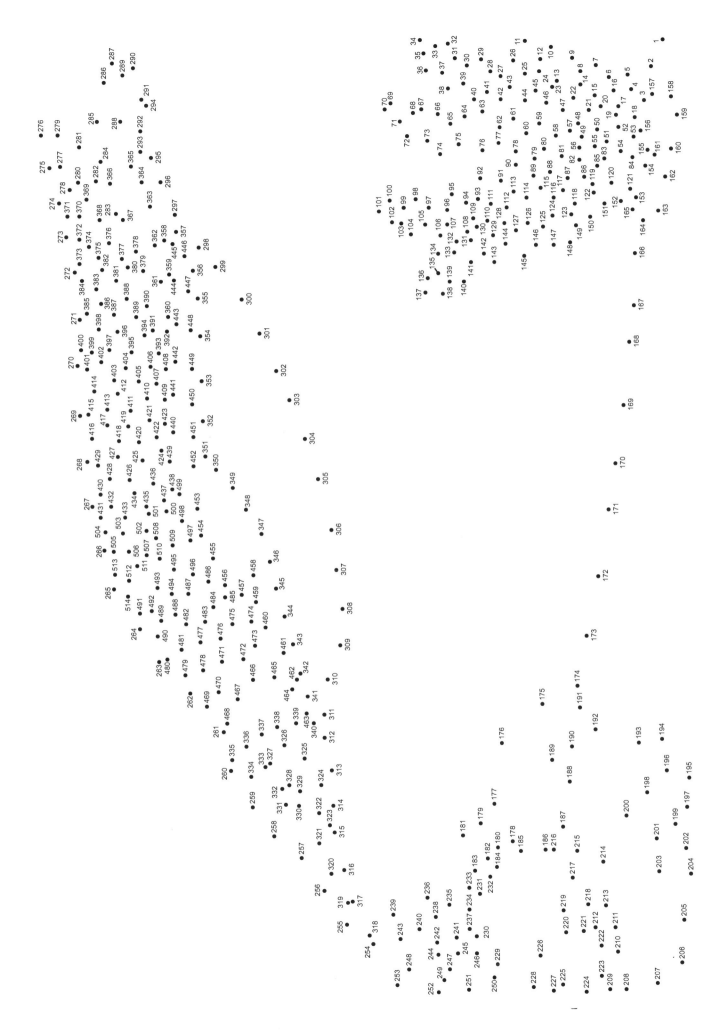

Penguin (514 dots) - Gray

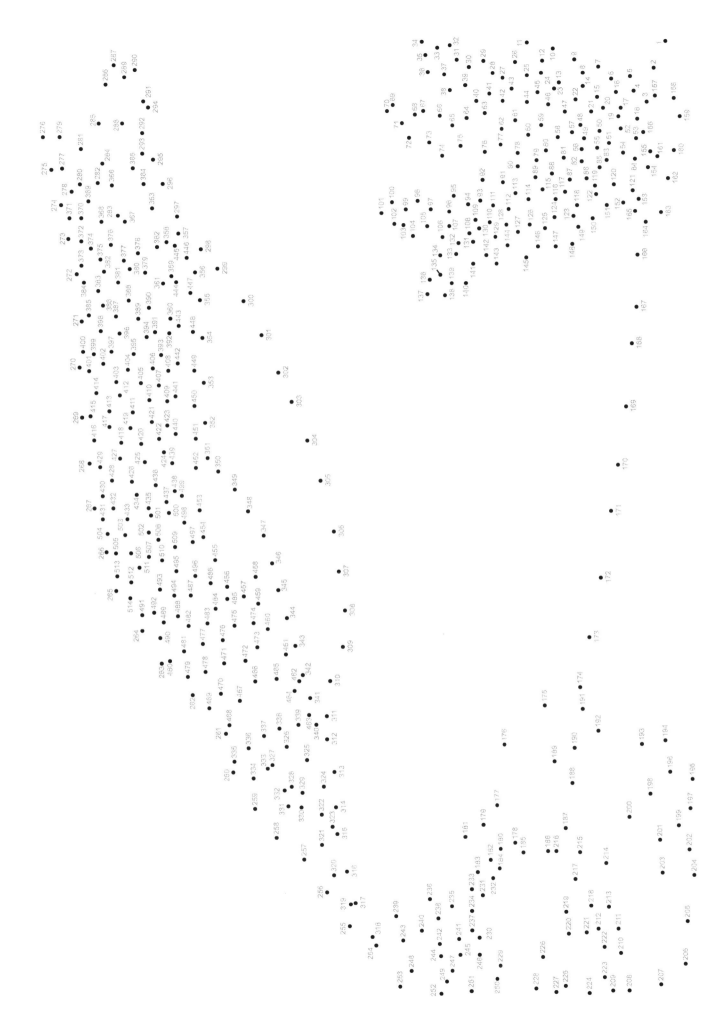

Pterophyllum Fish (678 dots) - Black

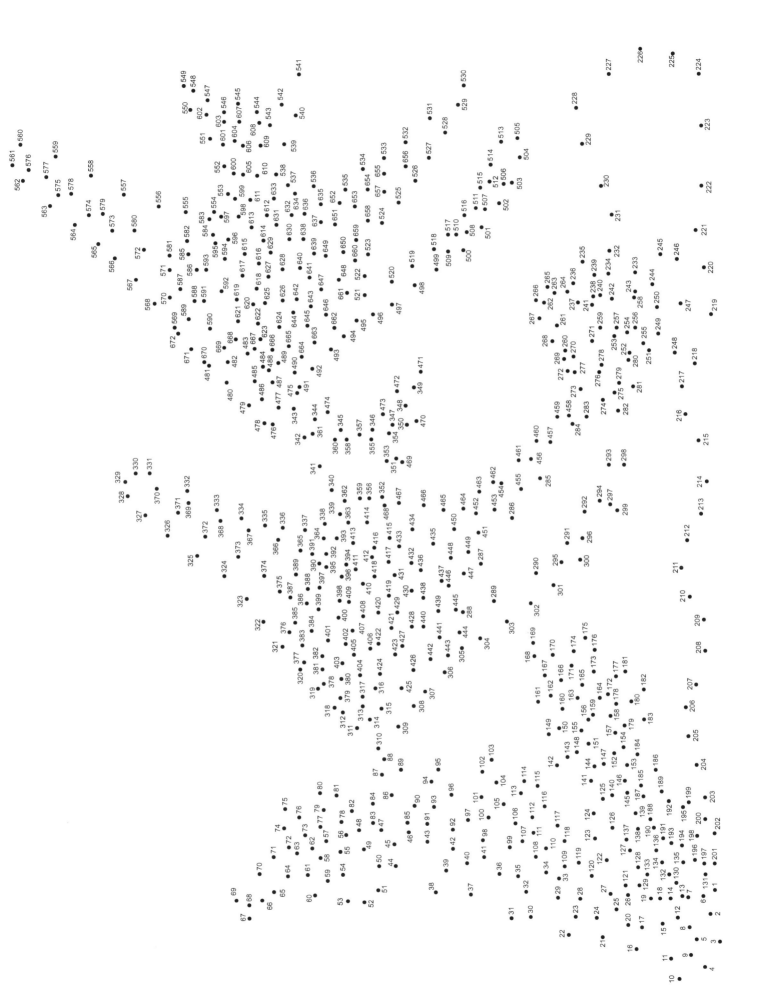

Pterophyllum Fish (678 dots) - Gray

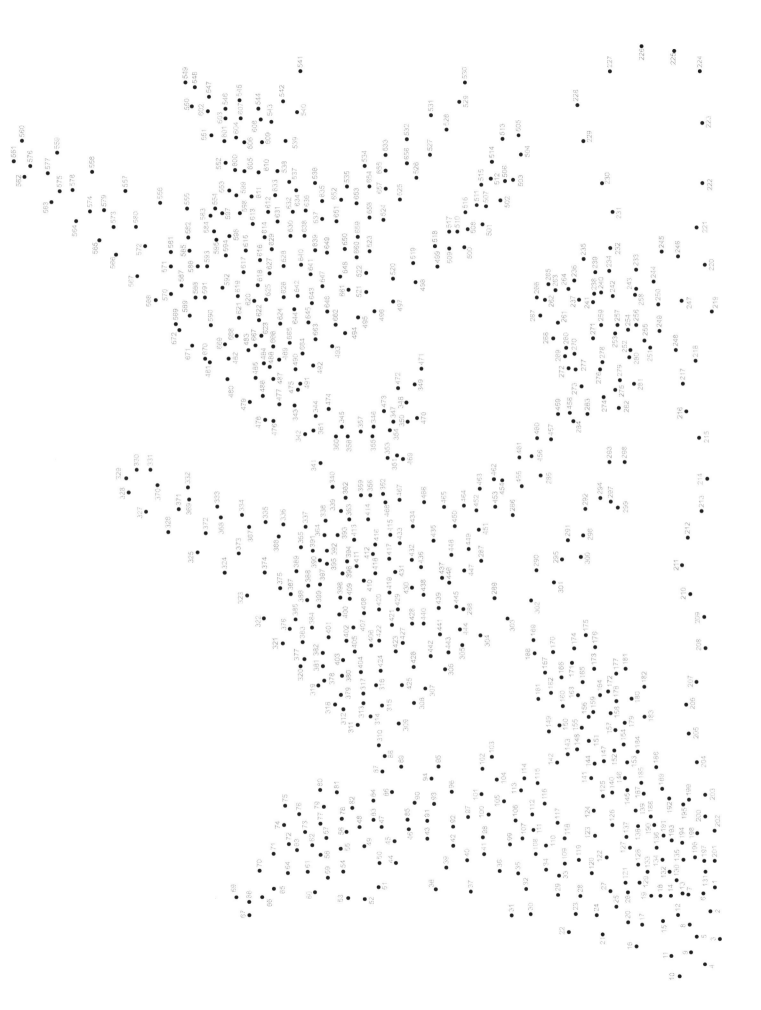

Sea Lion (427 dots) - Black

Sea Lion (427 dots) - Gray

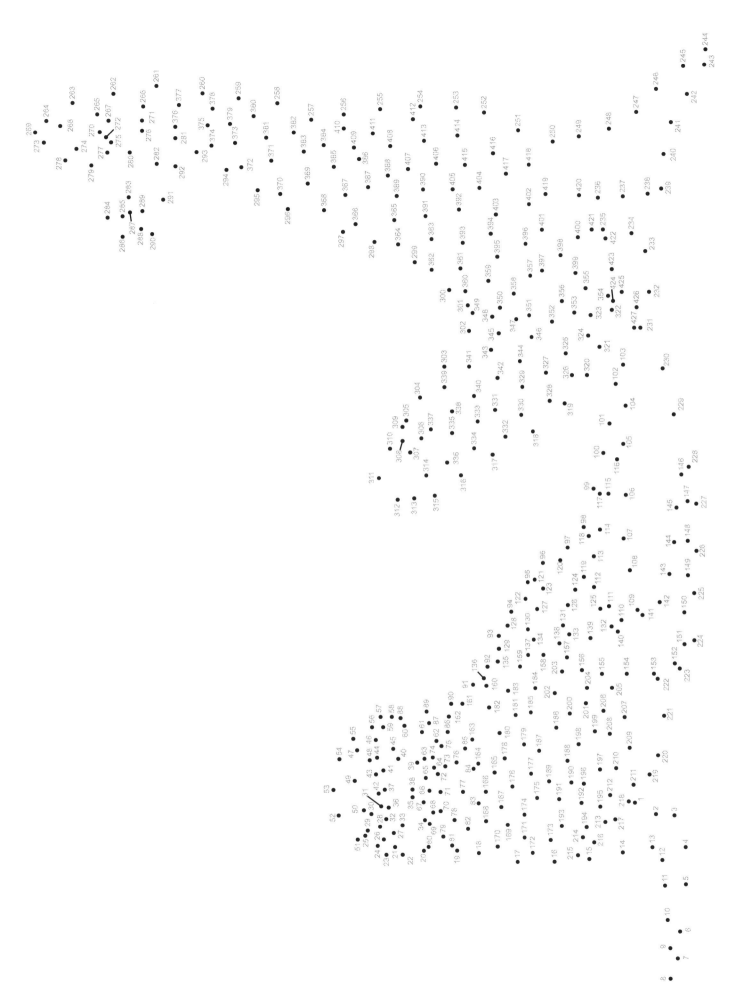

Sea Urchin (500 dots) - Black

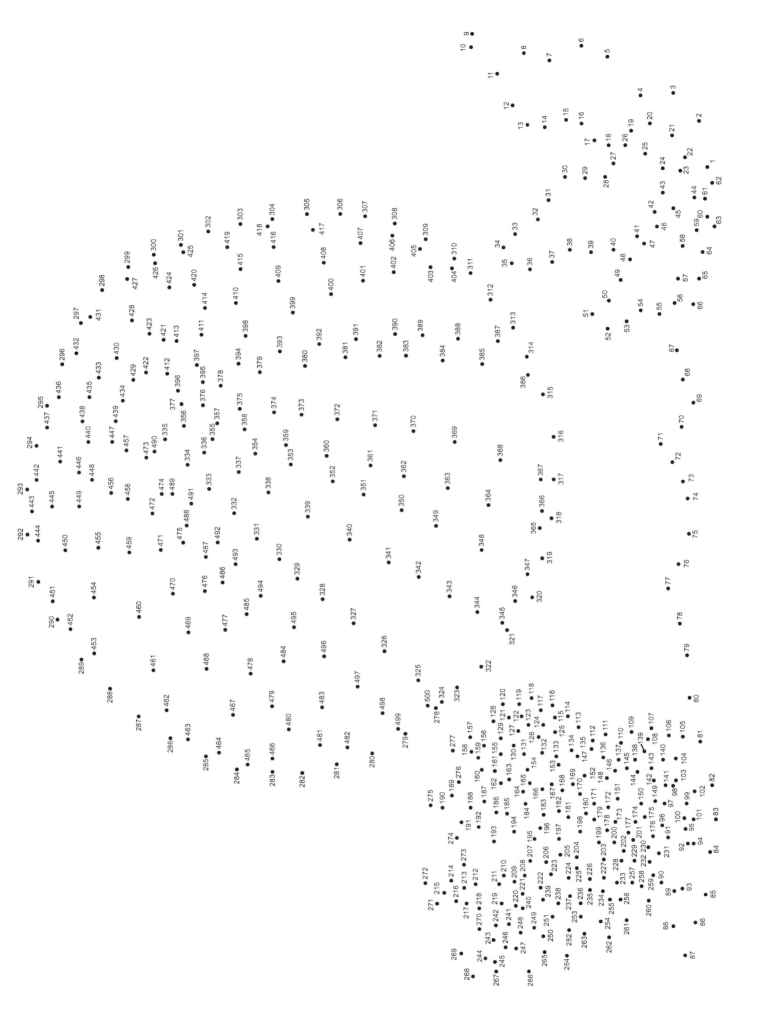

Sea Urchin (500 dots) - Gray

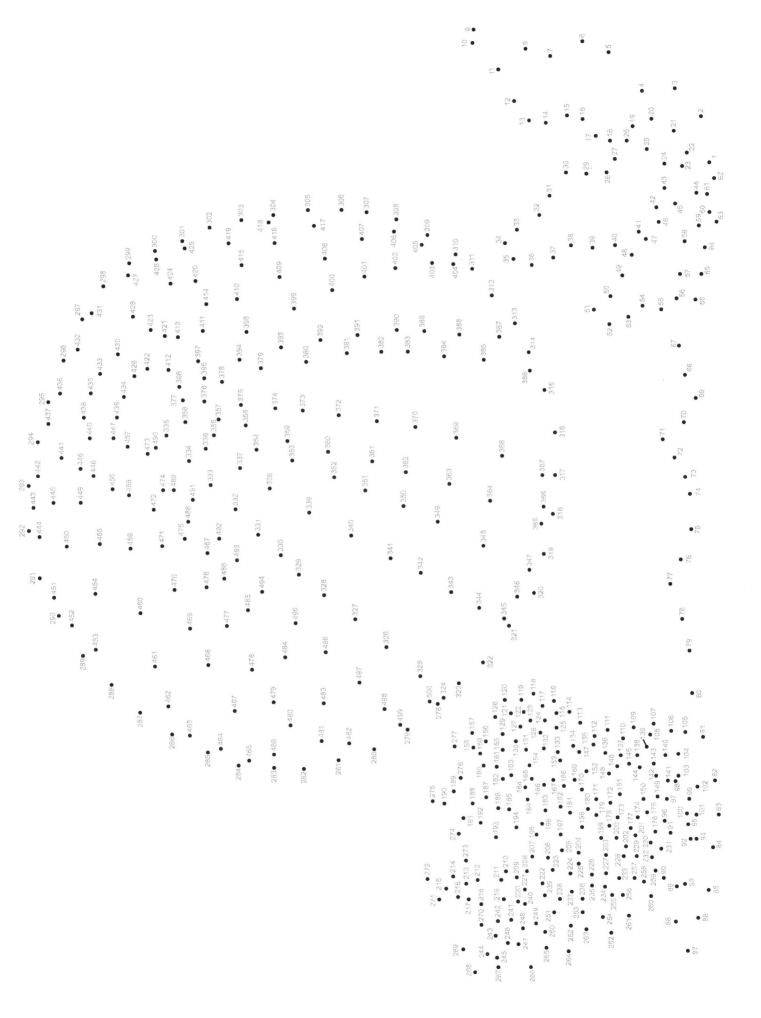

Seahorse (556 dots) - Black

Seahorse (556 dots) - Gray

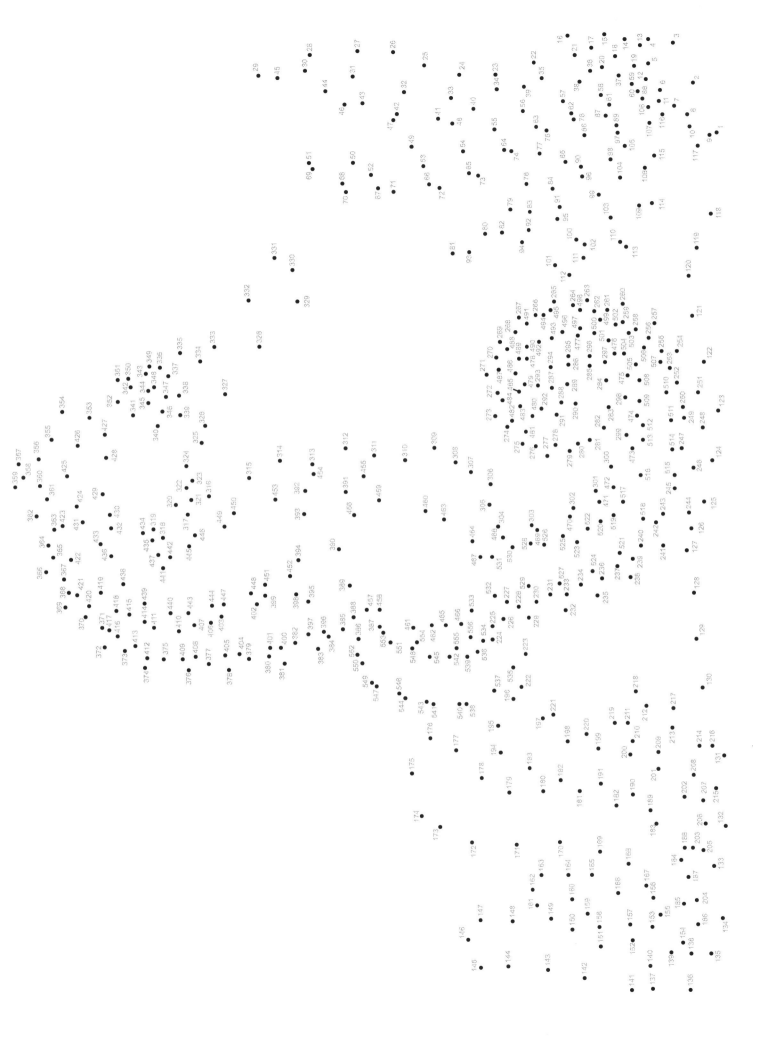

Seal (408 dots) - Black

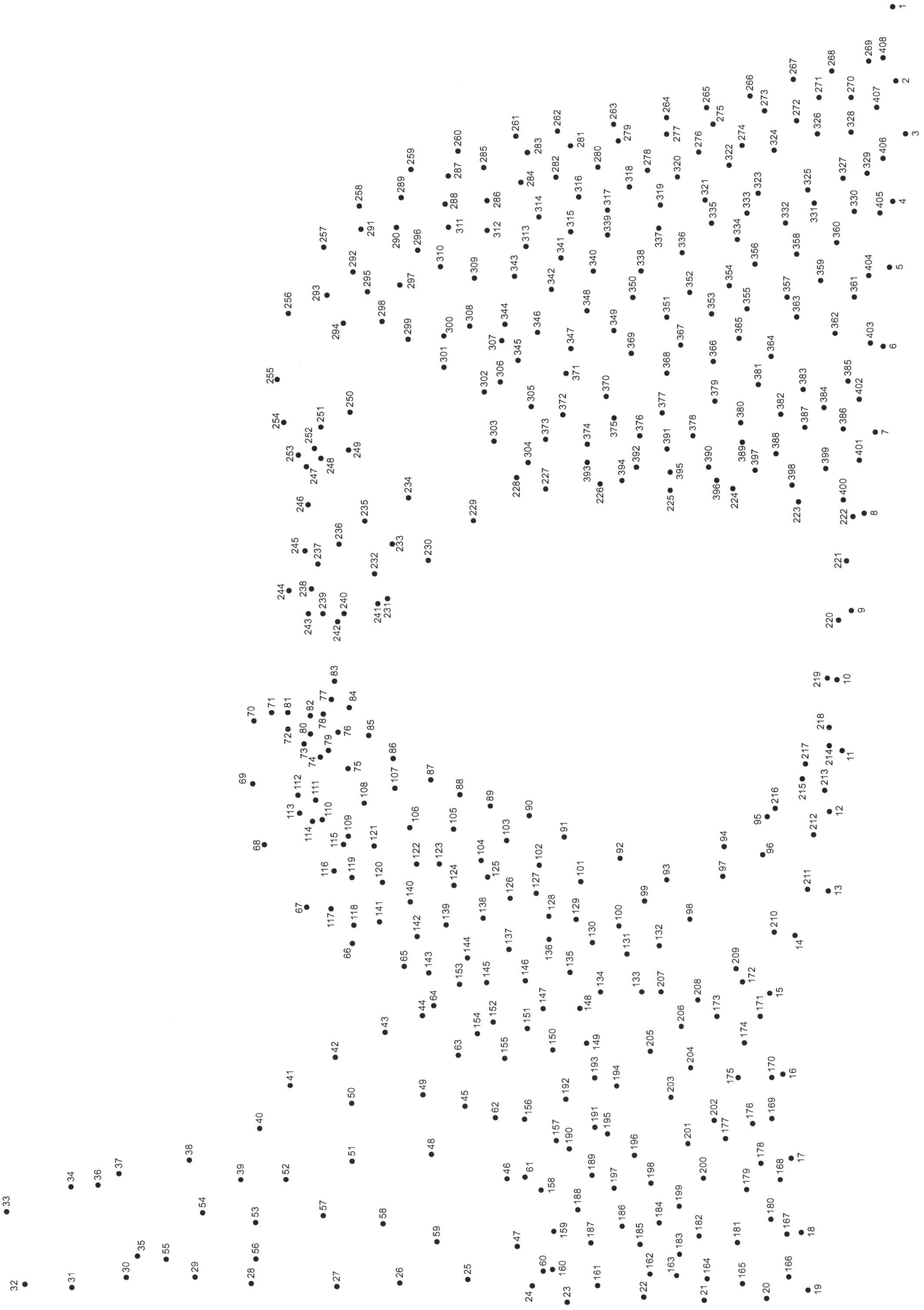

Seal (408 dots) - Gray

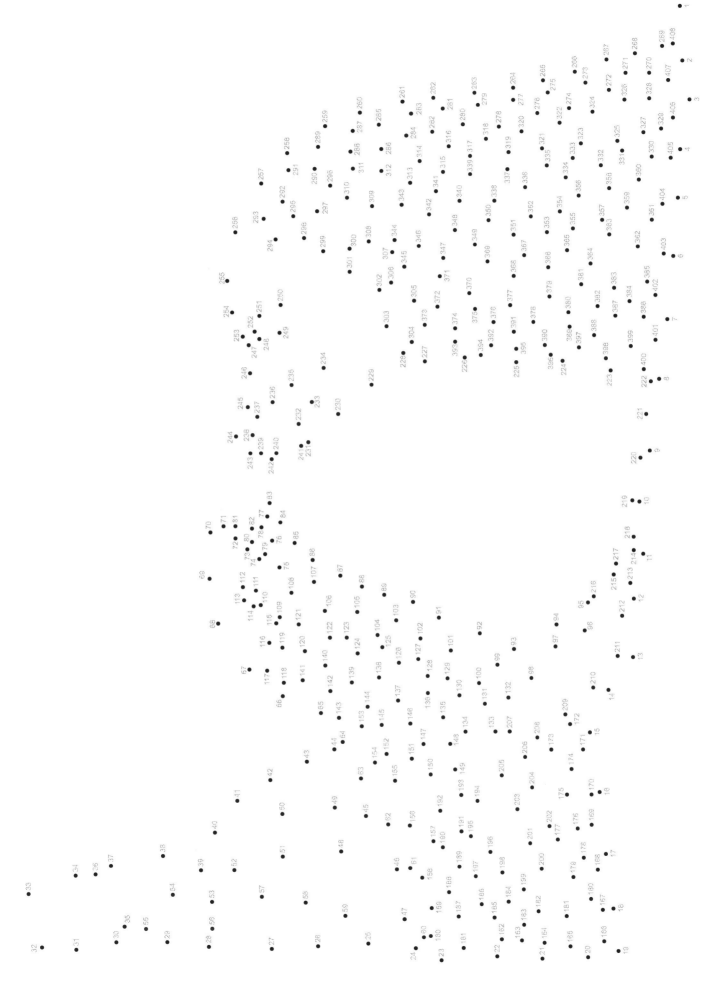

Shark (611 dots) - Black

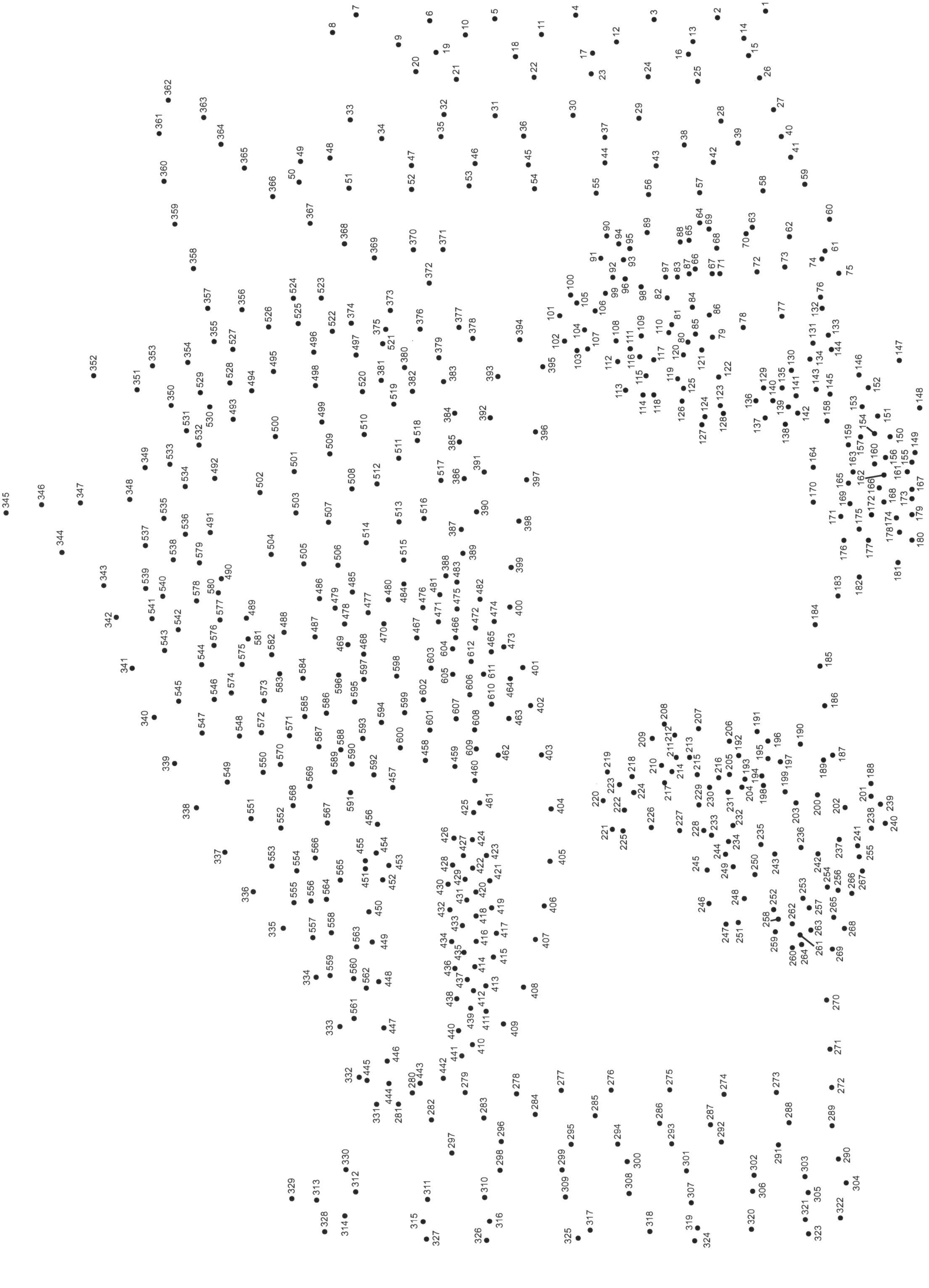

Shark (611 dots) - Black

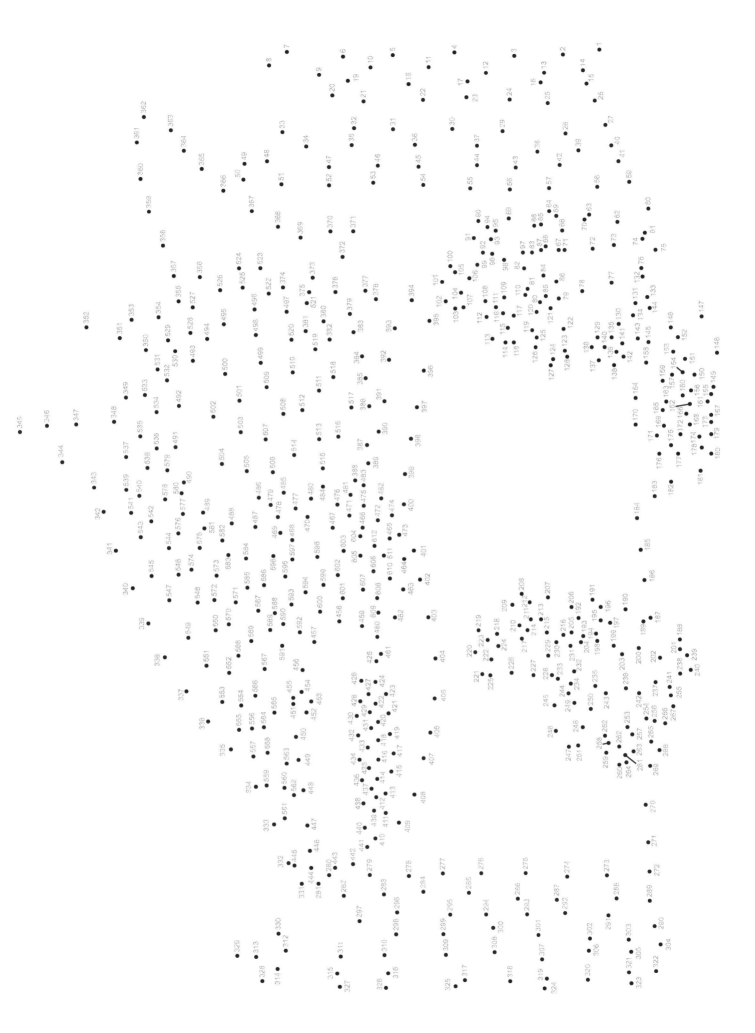

Shrimp (561 dots) - Black

Shrimp (561 dots) - Gray

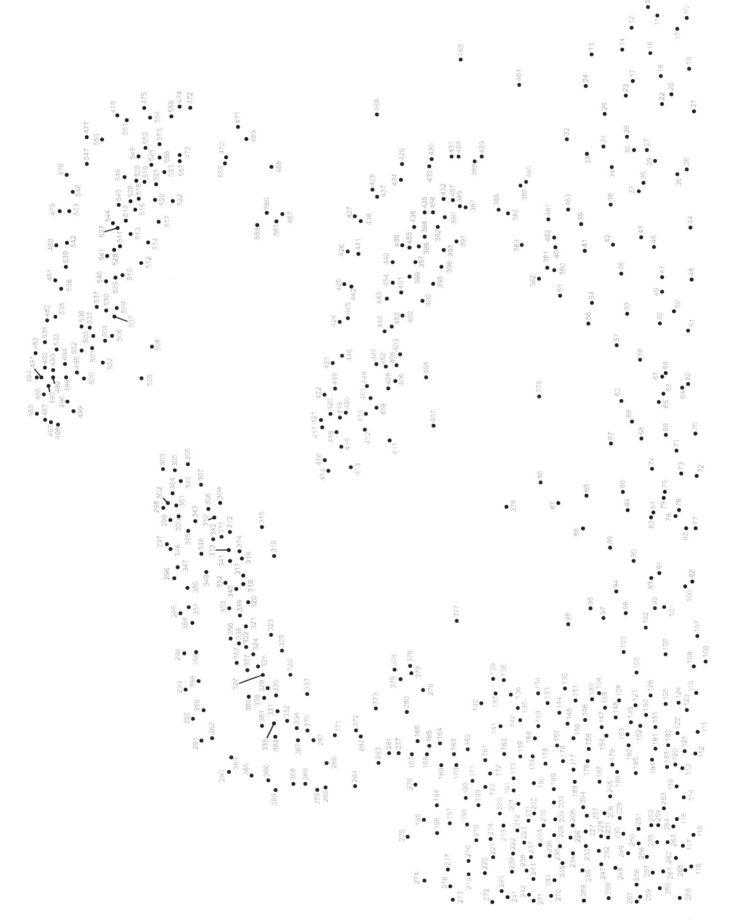

Starfish (487 dots) - Black

Starfish (487 dots) - Gray

Swordfish (582 dots) - Black

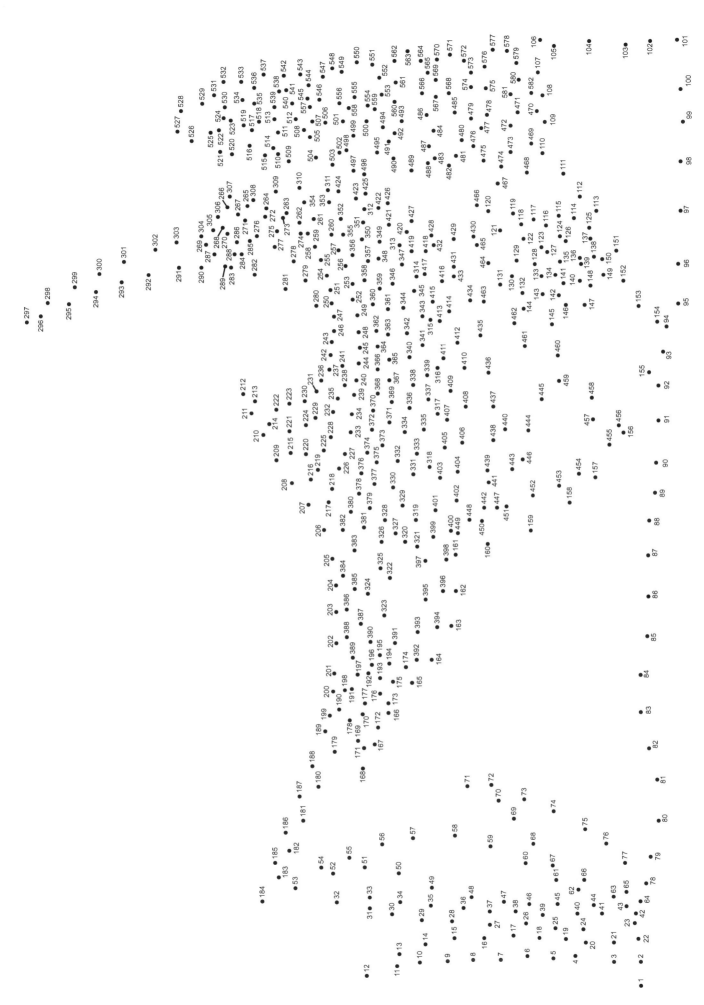

Swordfish (582 dots) - Gray

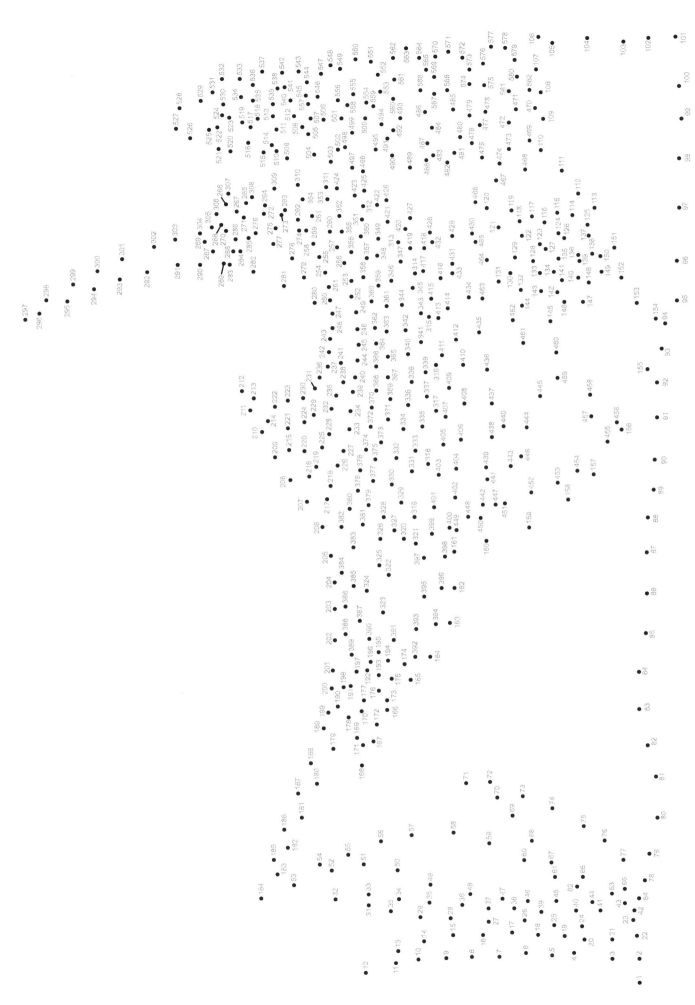

Tortoise (460 dots) - Black

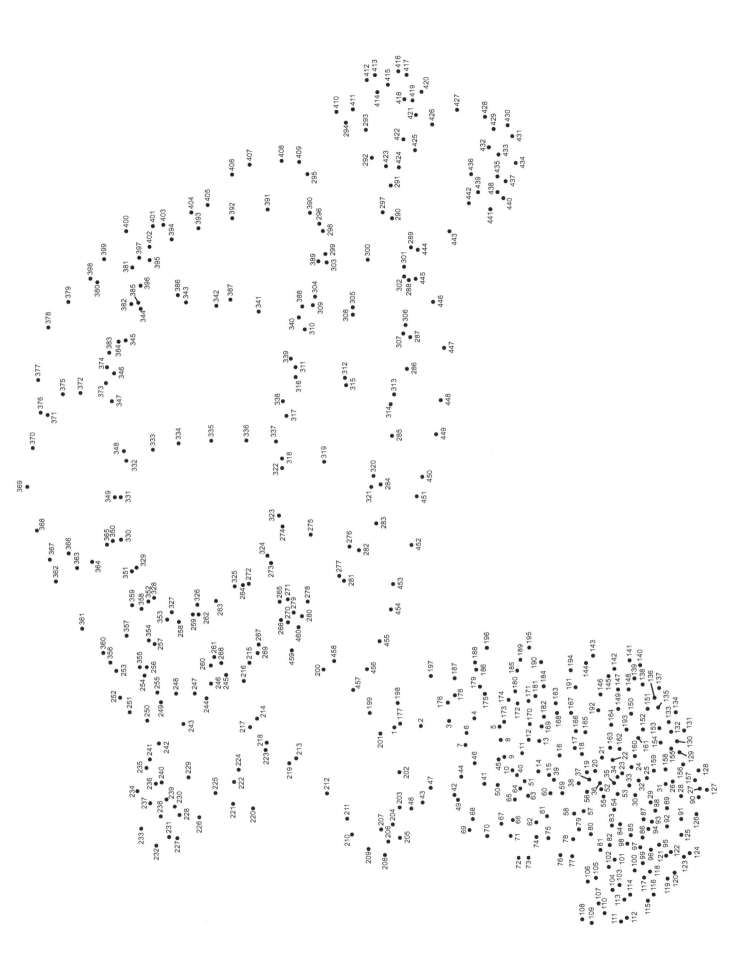

Tortoise (460 dots) - Gray

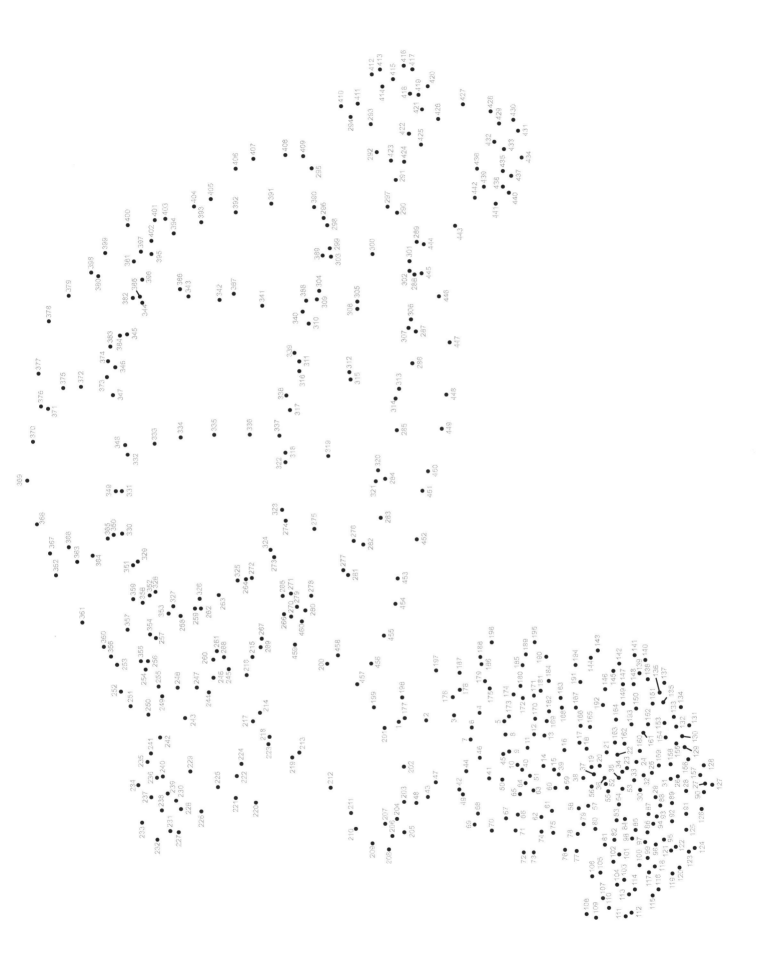

Walrus (392 dots) - Black

Walrus (392 dots) - Gray

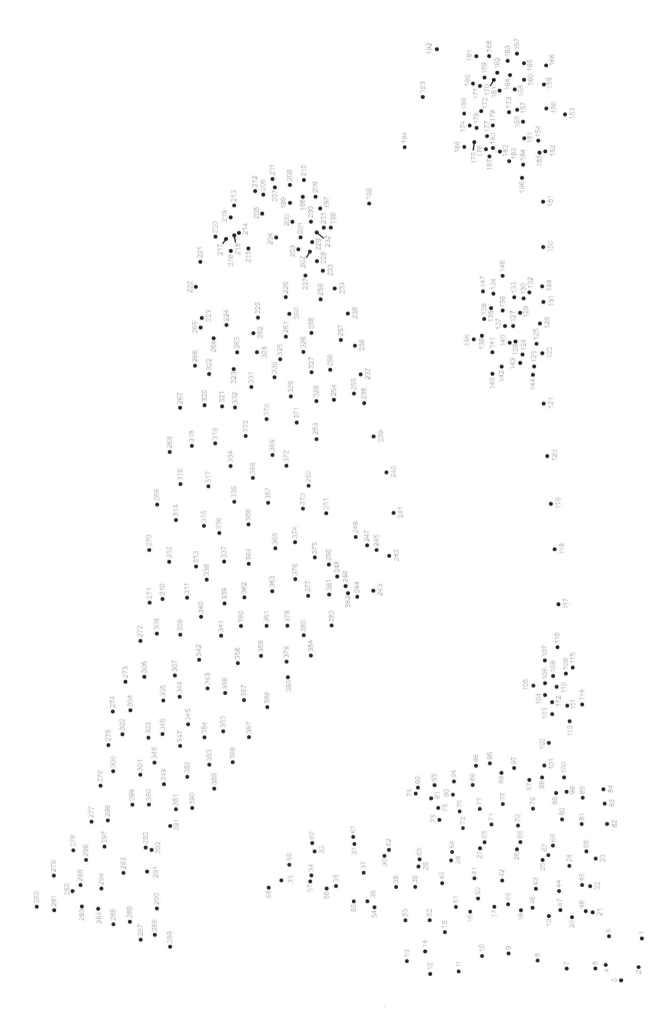

Whale (449 dots) - Black

Whale (449 dots) - Gray

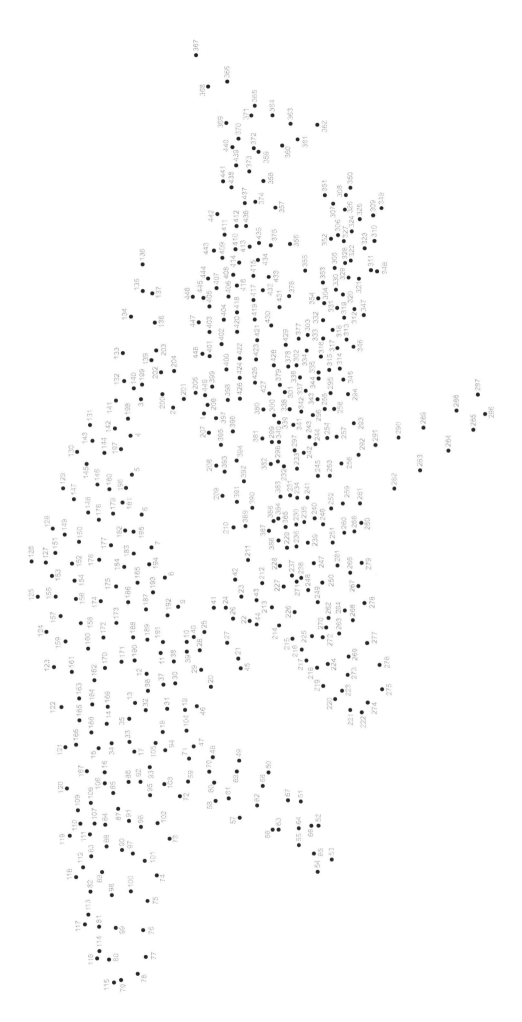

COMPELTED
DOT PAGES PREVIEWS

Completed Dot to Dot Pages Previews

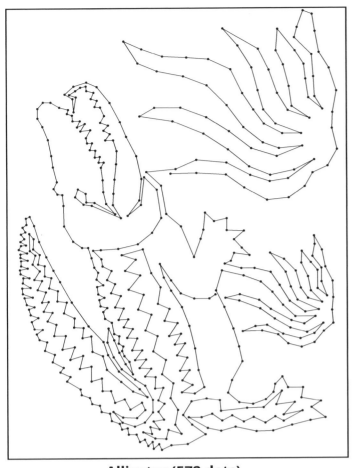

Alligator (572 dots) -

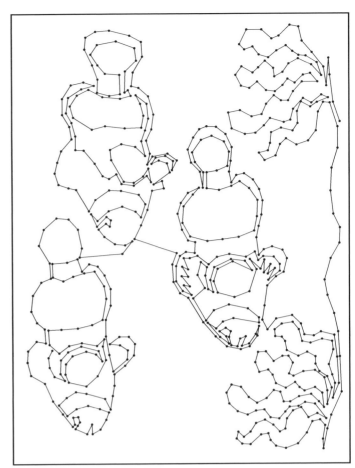

Clownfish (610 dots) -

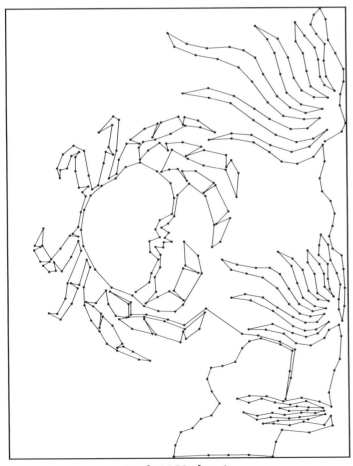

Crab (460 dots) -

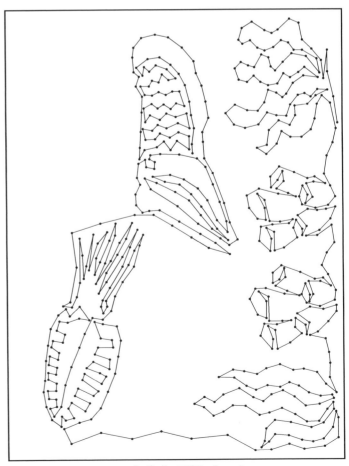

Cuttlefish (571 dots) -

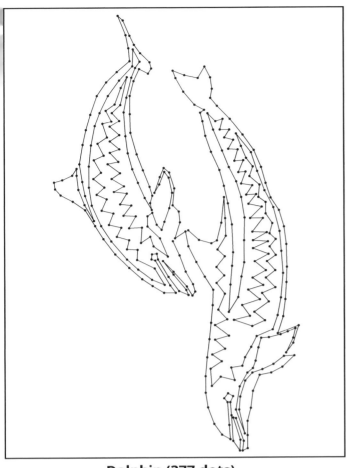

Dolphin (377 dots) -

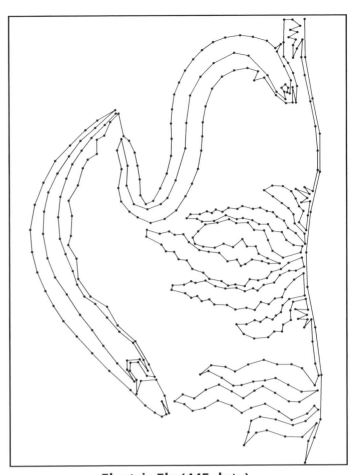

Electric Ele (445 dots) -

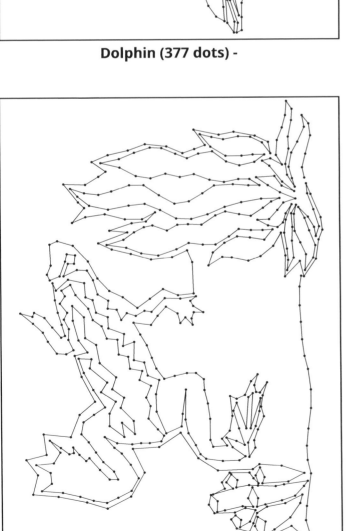

Frog (555 dots) -

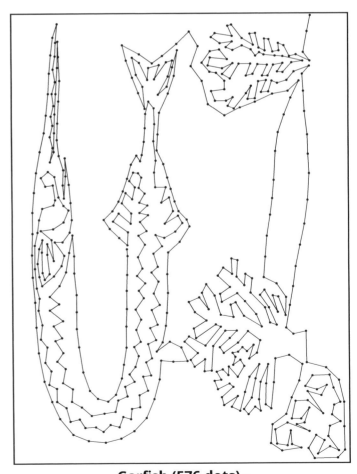

Garfish (576 dots) -

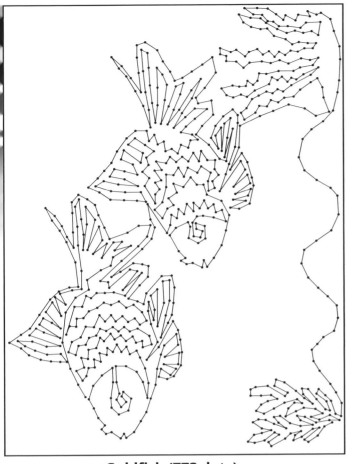

Goldfish (773 dots) -

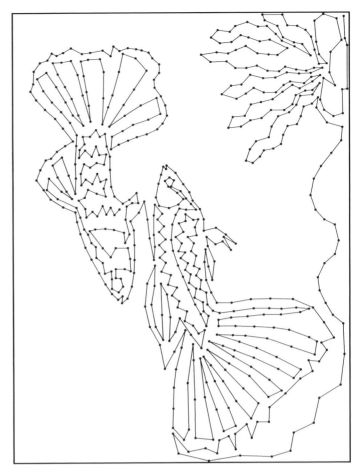

Guppy (612 dots) -

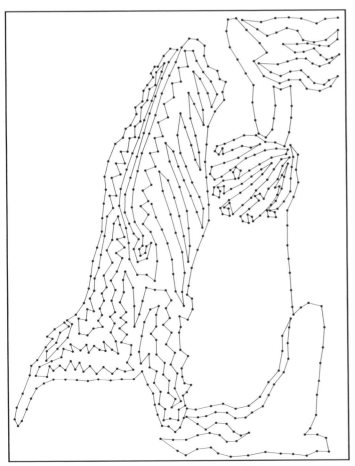

Humpback Whale (656 dots) -

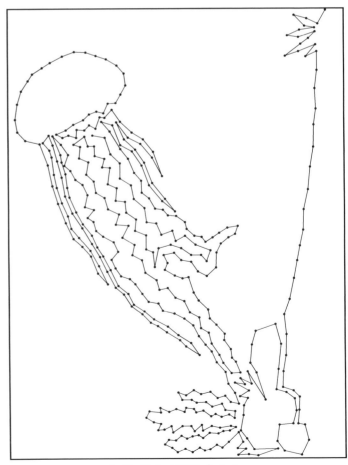

Jellyfish (420 dots) -

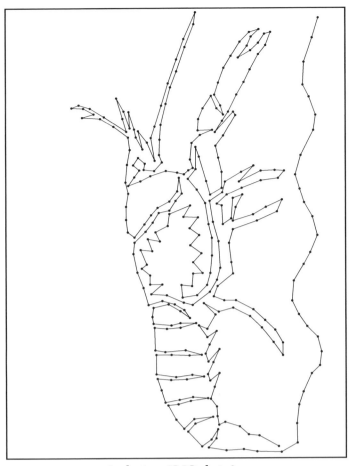

Lobster (313 dots) -

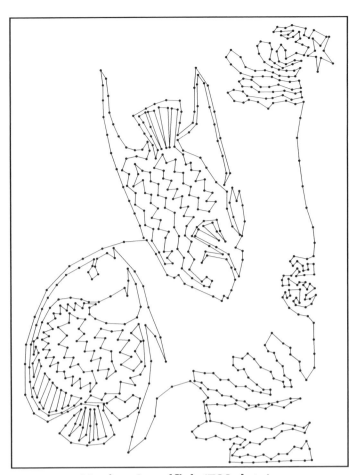

Marine Angelfish (728 dots) -

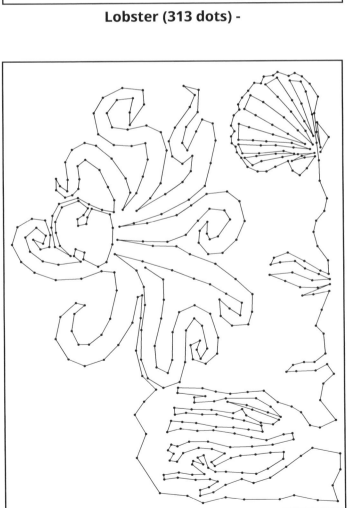

Octopus (483 dots) -

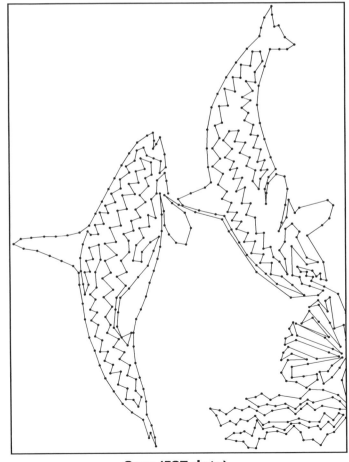

Orca (537 dots) -

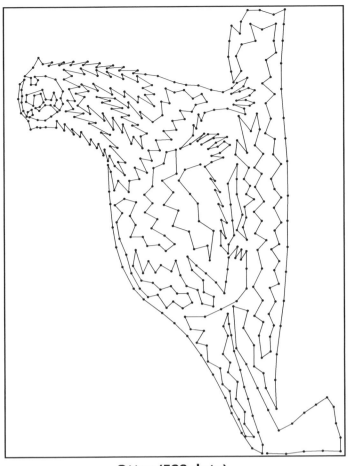

Otter (528 dots) -

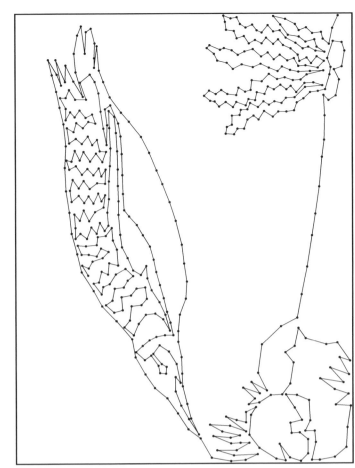

Penguin (514 dots) -

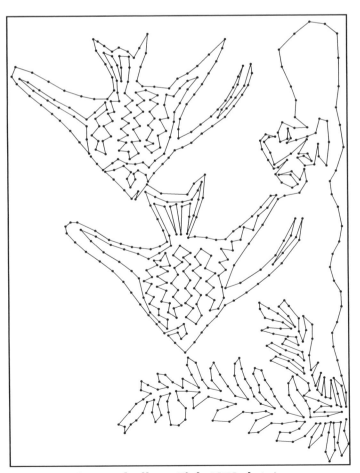

Pterophyllum Fish (678 dots) -

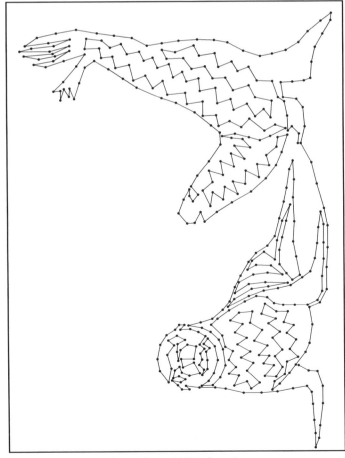

Sea Lion (427 dots) -

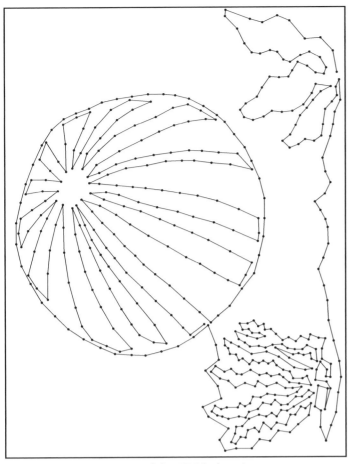

Sea Urchin (500 dots) -

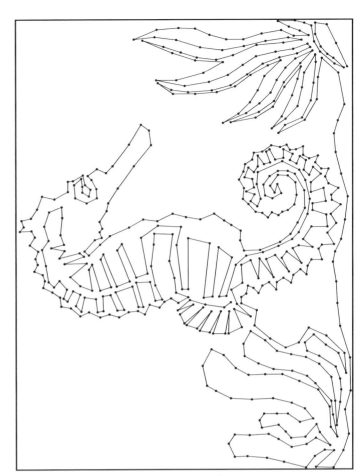

Seahorse (556 dots) -

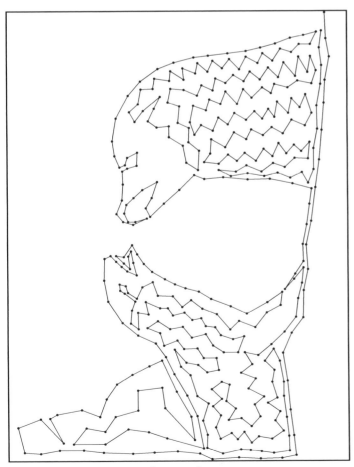

Seal (408 dots) -

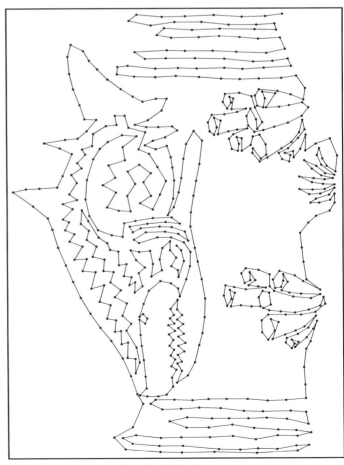

Shark (611 dots) -

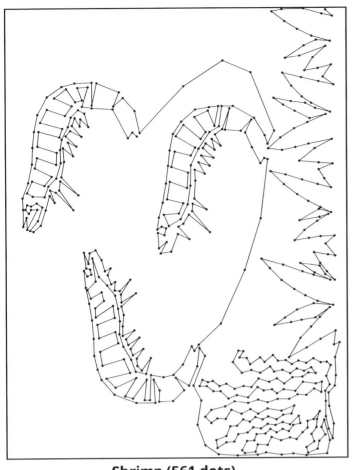

Shrimp (561 dots) -

Starfish (487 dots) -

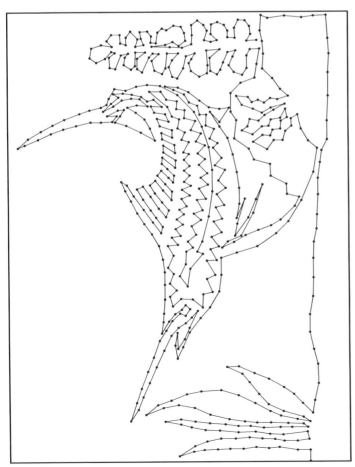

Swordfish (582 dots) -

Tortoise (460 dots) -

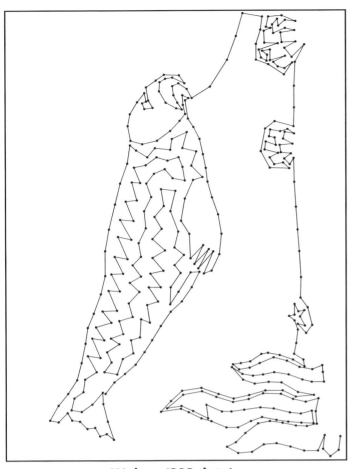

Walrus (392 dots) -

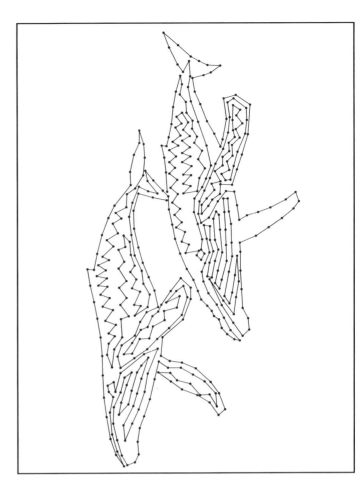

Whale (449 dots) -

Printed in Great Britain
by Amazon

More Dot to Dot Books for Adults

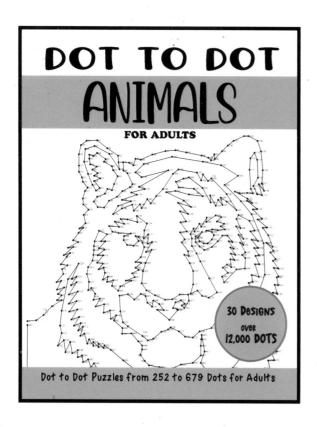

DOT TO DOT ANIMALS FOR ADULTS

30 Designs over 12,000 DOTS

Dot to Dot Puzzles from 252 to 679 Dots for Adults

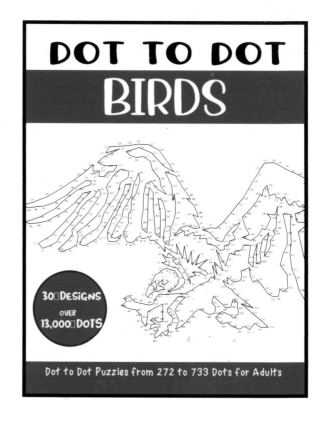

DOT TO DOT BIRDS

30 DESIGNS over 13,000 DOTS

Dot to Dot Puzzles from 272 to 733 Dots for Adults

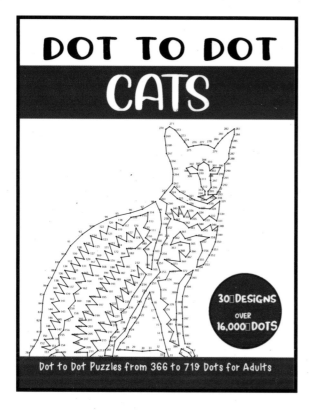

DOT TO DOT CATS

30 DESIGNS over 16,000 DOTS

Dot to Dot Puzzles from 366 to 719 Dots for Adults

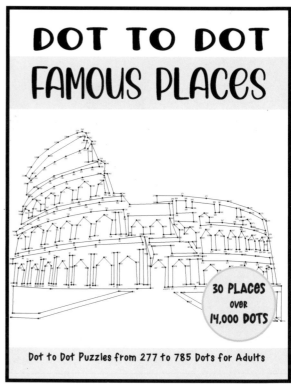

DOT TO DOT FAMOUS PLACES

30 PLACES over 14,000 DOTS

Dot to Dot Puzzles from 277 to 785 Dots for Adults

ISBN 9798549555310

9 798549 555310

90000